EDUCATION, CHRISTIANITY,
and
THE STATE

EDUCATION, CHRISTIANITY, and the STATE

J. Gresham Machen

Edited by John W. Robbins

The Trinity Foundation
Jefferson, Maryland

Cover: *Rural Schoolroom* by Perkins Harnly, *Index of American Design*, National Gallery of Art, Washington, D.C.

Education, Christianity, and the State
© 1987 The Trinity Foundation
Post Office Box 169
Jefferson, Maryland 21755
Library of Congress Card Number:
Printed in the United States of America
ISBN: 0-940931-19-2

Contents

Foreword vii

1. Faith and Knowledge 1
2. The Importance of Christian Scholarship 13
3. Christianity and Culture 45
4. Reforming the Government Schools 60
5. The Necessity of the Christian School 66
6. Shall We Have a Federal Department of Education? 84
7. Proposed Department of Education 99
8. The Christian School: The Hope of America 124
9. Westminster Theological Seminary: Its Purpose and Plan . . 145

Scripture Index 156
Index 157
The Crisis of Our Time 164
Intellectual Ammunition 173

Books by J. Gresham Machen

Christianity and Liberalism
The Christian Faith in the Modern World
The Christian View of Man
God Transcendent
The New Testament: An Introduction to Its Literature
    and History
New Testament Greek for Beginners
The Origin of Paul's Religion
The Virgin Birth of Christ
What is Christianity?
What Is Faith?

Foreword

Every century has had a shortage of Christian scholars, but the intellectual poverty of the twentieth century has been severe. The great names in Christian theology—John Calvin, Martin Luther, Augustine, Jonathan Edwards, Athanasius, John Owen, Charles Hodge—all belong to other times. It is not that we lack religious leaders or religious books, but that most of the religious leaders and books of the twentieth century have been either less than scholarly or less than Christian.

There is a reason for this. In the last third of the eighteenth century secular philosophers launched a frenetic and strident attack on man's intellect. Theologians soon joined the attack, an assault that has now been sustained for two centuries. Immanuel Kant, Soren Kierkegaard, Friedrich Schleiermacher, Friedrich Nietzsche, Karl Marx, and the Romantic movement were early aggressors; in this century they have been reinforced by the pragmatists, the existentialists, the positivists, the neo-orthodox, and the liberals. Soren Kierkegaard, the Danish theologian, declared in the early nineteenth century: "It was intelligence and nothing else that had to be opposed. Presumably that is why I, who had the job, was armed with an immense intelligence."

It is this anti-intellectualism that has caused the mediocrity of Christian scholarship, education, and leadership in the twentieth century. Rather than rejecting this anti-Christian view, the professing church has been heavily influenced and even overcome by it. The modern church has substituted feelings and "love" for knowledge and doctrine. According to modern theology, the intellect cannot be trusted, but the emotions can. The intellect has been affected by sin, but the emotions have not. A false distinction, latent in popular religion for decades, occupies a central place in twentieth century religion: the alleged distinction between the head and the heart.

To smuggle in their new religion while still retaining Biblical language, modern theologians have quietly redefined Biblical terms. The process began with words like *divinity* and *infallibility,* but it has spread much further than most people suspect. *Heart,* which in the Bible means the inner man, the self, the mind, now means the seat of the emotions. Modern theology contrasts the heart with the head, something the Bible never does. *Love,* which the Bible defines as obedience to God's moral law, is now a feeling. *Knowledge,* which in the Bible is propositional truth received by the mind, is now something experiential. Intellectual knowledge, contemporary theologians warn, leads only to pride, and is to be avoided at all costs. *Faith,* which in the Bible means either believing something to be true, or the propositions believed, is now a leap in the dark; it is trusting or encountering a person, not believing a proposition to be true. Propositional truth has been replaced by an undefinable and indescribable personal "truth."

Some alert Christians realize that a redefinition of Biblical terms has taken place in the twentieth century, and they have objected to some of the new definitions. At the beginning of the twentieth century, it was no longer enough for Christians to speak of the divinity of Christ, for the new meaning of *divinity* made every man divine. It became necessary to speak of the *deity* of Christ. Nor was it sufficient to affirm that the Bible *contains* the Word of God, for *contains* was redefined to mean that the Bible also contains words of human origin. During the latter half of the twentieth century it is no longer sufficient to say that the Bible is *infallible;* now one must say that it is *inerrant,* for *infallible* has been redefined by the modern theologians to mean *fallible.*

While many Christians have understood the subversive nature of the new definitions, they have failed to understand that the process of redefining Biblical terms has progressed far beyond the words *divinity, contain,* and *infallibility.* They do not realize that Kant, Schleiermacher, Kierkegaard, and their many disciples have changed the fundamental meaning of Christianity itself, locating it not in the intellect, but in the feelings.

It is this notion, so thoroughly unscriptural and so completely subversive of Christianity, that has left the Christian church of the twentieth century bereft of intellectual leadership. J. Gresham Machen understood the meaning of this modern anti-intellectualism quite well. He wrote one book, *Christianity and Liberalism,* to call attention to the new religion which was quickly and quietly replacing Christianity in the churches by using Christian terms with new meanings. He wrote another book, *What Is Faith?* for the purpose of combatting modern anti-intellectualism in one area, the nature of faith. In *What Is Faith?* Machen wrote:

> The anti-intellectual tendency in the modern world is no trifling thing; it has its root deep in the entire philosophical development of modern times. Modern philosophy since the days of Kant, with the theology that has been influenced by it, has had as its dominant note, certainly as its present-day result, a depreciation of the reason and a skeptical answer to Pilate's question, "What is truth?" This attack upon the intellect has been conducted by men of marked intellectual power; but an attack upon the intellect it has been all the same. And at last the logical results of it, even in the sphere of practice, are beginning

to appear. A marked characteristic of the present day is a lamentable intellectual decline, which has appeared in all fields of human endeavor except those that deal with purely material things. The intellect has been browbeaten so long in theory that one cannot be surprised if it is now ceasing to function in practice.

The demise of Christian intellectualism in the twentieth century is a tragedy of major proportions. It is doubly tragic because Christian laymen, harassed by both Church and State, have been largely abandoned by the leadership in the churches. Laymen, educating their children both at home and in Christian schools, realize that Christian education is and must be an intellectual affair; and just when the leadership of Christian intellectuals is most needed, the laymen have been deserted.

Christian leaders have vigorously opposed intellectual endeavors. They have separated knowledge and spirituality and made them into enemies. The un-Biblical antithesis between the head and the heart is incompatible with Christian education. Christian laymen have begun to realize that Christian education cannot long endure without an intellectual foundation, and that foundation cannot be found in modern theology of any variety, liberal or "conservative."

The theological foundation for Christian education is Biblical Christianity alone. In this book, J. Gresham Machen sketches the outlines of that theology; in *A Christian Philosophy of Education* Gordon H. Clark presents the full philosophical and theological statement.

Like Clark, J. Gresham Machen was one of the few Christian intellectuals of this century. It is a tragedy that in the fifty years since Machen's death no edition of his collected writings has been published.[1] His respect for independent

---

1. Unfortunately the institutions Machen founded have been influenced by modern

thinking, for thorough education, and for scholarship is amply displayed in the essays that follow. His ideas, along with those of Gordon H. Clark in *A Christian Philosophy of Education*, furnish the indispensable theological and philosophical foundation for Christian education. If the Christian school and home schooling movements are to succeed in educating Christian men who can challenge the world at every level, in every discipline, and win, it will only be because they have adopted the ideas expressed by Machen and Clark.

J. Gresham Machen died fifty years ago on January 1, 1937. He was praised in his death by believer and unbeliever alike. H.L. Mencken praised him for "his remarkable clarity and cogency as an apologist." Pearl S. Buck, a novelist and one of his modernist opponents in the Presbyterian Church, described him as "admirable. He never gave in one inch to anyone. He never bowed his head. It was not in him to trim or compromise, to accept any peace that was less than triumph. He was a glorious enemy because he was completely open and direct in his angers and hatreds. He stood for something and everyone knew what it was." C.W. Hodge of Princeton Seminary, whose faculty Machen had left seven years earlier in order to found a new Christian seminary, "regarded him as the greatest theologian in the English-speaking world. The whole cause of evangelical Christianity has lost its greatest leader."

Machen is in heaven, but his writings are still with us. By reprinting these essays, we are honoring one of the few

---

irrationalism and have found his emphasis on and defense of the intellect hard to swallow. For example, in the large volume of essays commemorating the semi-centennial of the Orthodox Presbyterian Church, only two of thirty essays discuss Machen's indispensable role in that Church's history, and one of them, by far the longer, is a strained attempt to show how Machen's Christian intellectualism is compatible with Cornelius Van Til's irrationalism. The line of philosophical and theological descent from Machen waned in that Church, being replaced by various forms of irrationalism, but it has continued in the work of Gordon H. Clark and his students.

Christian scholars of the twentieth century, and advancing the cause of Christianity and Christian education at the same time. We are commanded by God not to be conformed to this world, but to be transformed by the renewing of our minds. To accomplish that renewing, God has given us a book of sixty-six books containing thousands of propositions to read, study, understand, remember, and believe. It is our *minds* that both God demands and the world deforms. Machen understood that lesson quite well. May we, through the grace of God, come to that same understanding.

John W. Robbins
August 12, 1987

1

Faith and Knowledge*

The question, "What is Faith?", which forms the subject of the following discussion may seem to some persons impertinent and unnecessary. Faith, it may be said, cannot be known except by experience, and when it is known by experience logical analysis of it, and logical separation of it from other experience, will only serve to destroy its power and its charm. The man who knows by experience what it is to trust Christ, for example, to rest upon Him for salvation, will never need, it may be held, to engage in psychological investigations of that experience which is the basis of his life; and indeed such investigations may even serve to destroy the thing that is to be investigated.

Such objections are only one manifestation of a tendency that is very widespread at the present day, the tendency to disparage the intellectual aspect of the religious life. Religion, it is held, is an ineffable experience; the intellectual expression of it can be symbolical merely; the most various opinions in the religious sphere are compatible with a fundamental unity of life; theology may vary and yet religion may remain the same.

Obviously this temper of mind is hostile to precise definitions. Indeed nothing makes a man more unpopular in the controversies of the present day than an insistence upon definition of terms. Anything, it seems, may be forgiven more

---

readily than that. Men discourse very eloquently today upon such subjects as God, religion, Christianity, atonement, redemption, faith; but are greatly incensed when they are asked to tell in simple language what they mean by these terms. They do not like to have the flow of their eloquence checked by so vulgar a thing as a definition. And so they will probably be incensed by the question which forms the title of the present book; in the midst of eloquent celebrations of faith—usually faith contrasted with knowledge—it seems disconcerting to be asked what faith is.

This anti-intellectual tendency in the modern world is no trifling thing; it has its roots deep in the entire philosophical development of modern times. Modern philosophy since the days of Kant, with the theology that has been influenced by it, has had as its dominant note, certainly as its present-day result, a depreciation of the reason and a skeptical answer to Pilate's question, "What is truth?" This attack upon the intellect has been conducted by men of marked intellectual power; but an attack upon the intellect it has been all the same. And at last the logical results of it, even in the sphere of practice, are beginning to appear. A marked characteristic of the present day is a lamentable intellectual decline, which has appeared in all fields of human endeavor except those that deal with purely material things. The intellect has been browbeaten so long in theory that one cannot be surprised if it is now ceasing to function in practice. Schleiermacher and Ritschl, despite their own intellectual gifts, have, it may fairly be maintained, contributed largely to produce that indolent impressionism which, for example in the field of New Testament studies, has largely taken the place of the patient researches of a generation or so ago.

The intellectual decadence of the day is not limited to the Church, or to the subject of religion, but appears in secular education as well. Sometimes it is assisted by absurd pedagogic theories, which, whatever their variety in detail, are alike in their depreciation of the labor of learning facts. Facts, in the sphere of education, are having a hard time. The old-fashioned notion of reading a book and hearing a lecture and simply storing up in the mind what the book or the lecture contains —this is regarded as entirely out of date. A year or so ago I heard a noted educator give some advice to a company of college professors—advice which was typical of the present tendency in education. It is a great mistake, he said in effect, to suppose that a college professor ought to teach; on the contrary he ought simply to give the students an opportunity to learn.

This pedagogic theory of following the line of least resistance in education and avoiding all drudgery and all hard work has been having its natural result; it has joined forces with the natural indolence of youth to produce in present-day education a very lamentable decline.

The decline has not, indeed, been universal; in the sphere of the physical sciences, for example, the acquisition of facts is not regarded as altogether out of date. Indeed, the anti-intellectualistic tendency in religion and in those subjects that deal specifically with the things of the spirit has been due, partly at least, to a monopolistic possession of the intellect on the part of the physical sciences and of their utilitarian applications. But in the long run it is to be questioned whether even those branches of endeavor will profit by their monopolistic claims; in the long run the intellect will hardly profit by being excluded from the higher interests of the human spirit, and its decadence may then appear even in the material sphere.

But however that may be, whether or not intellectual decadence has already extended or will soon extend to the physical sciences, its prevalence in other spheres—in literature and history, for example, and still more clearly in the study of language—is perfectly plain. An outstanding feature of contemporary education in these spheres is the growth of ignorance; pedagogic theory and the growth of ignorance have gone hand in hand.

The undergraduate student of the present day is being told that he need not take notes on what he hears in class, that the exercise of the memory is a rather childish and mechanical thing, and that what he is really in college to do is to think for himself and to unify his world. He usually makes a poor business of unifying his world. And the reason is clear. He does not succeed in unifying his world for the simple reason that he has no world to unify. He has not acquired a knowledge of a sufficient number of facts in order even to learn the method of putting facts together. He is being told to practise the business of mental digestion; but the trouble is that he has no food to digest. The modern student, contrary to what is often said, is really being starved for want of facts.

Certainly we are not discouraging originality. On the contrary we desire to encourage it in every possible way, and we believe that the encouragement of it will be of immense benefit to the spread of the Christian religion. The trouble with the university students of the present day, from the point of view of evangelical Christianity, is not that they are too original, but that they are not half original enough. They go on in the same routine way, following their leaders like a flock of sheep, repeating the same stock phrases with little knowledge of what they mean, swallowing whole whatever professors choose to give them—and all the time imagining that they are bold, bad, independent young men, merely because they abuse what everybody else is abusing, namely, the religion that is founded upon Christ. It is popular today to abuse that unpopular thing that is known as supernatural Christianity, but original it certainly is not. A true originality might bring some resistance to the current of the age, some willingness to be unpopular, and some independent scrutiny, at least, if not acceptance, of the claims of Christ. If there is one thing more than another which we believers in historic Christianity ought to encourage in the youth of our day it is independence of mind.

It is a great mistake, then, to suppose that we who are called "conservatives" hold desperately to certain beliefs merely because they are old, and are opposed to the discovery of new facts. On the contrary, we welcome new discoveries with all our hearts, and we believe that our cause will come to its rights again only when youth throws off its present intellectual lethargy, refuses to go thoughtlessly with the anti-intellectual current of the age, and recovers some genuine independence of mind. In one sense, indeed, we are traditionalists; we do maintain that any institution that is really great has its roots in the past; we do not therefore desire to substitute modern sects for the historic Christian Church. But on the whole, in view of the conditions that now exist, it would perhaps be more correct to call us "radicals" than to call us "conservatives." We look not for a mere continuation of spiritual conditions that now exist, but for an outburst of new power; we are seeking in particular to arouse youth from its present uncritical repetition of current phrases into some genuine examination of the basis of life; and we believe that Christianity flourishes not in the darkness, but in the light. A revival of the Christian religion, we believe, will deliver mankind from its present bondage, and like the great revival of the sixteenth century will bring liberty to mankind. Such a revival will be not the work of man, but the work of the Spirit of God. But one of the means which the Spirit will use, we believe, is an awakening of the intellect. The retrograde, anti-intellectual movement called Modernism, a movement which really degrades the intellect by excluding it from the sphere of religion, will be overcome, and thinking will again come to its rights. The new Reformation, in other words, will be accompanied by a new Renaissance; and the last thing in the world that we desire to do is to discourage originality or independence of mind.

But what we do insist upon is that the right to originality has to be earned, and that it cannot be earned by ignorance or by indolence. A man cannot be original in his treatment of a subject unless he knows what the subject is; true originality is preceded by patient attention to the facts. It is that patient attention to the facts which, in application of modern pedagogic theory, is being neglected by the youth of the present day.

In our insistence upon mastery of facts in education, we are sometimes charged with the desire of forcing our opinions ready-made upon our students. We professors get up behind our professorial desks, it is said, and proceed to lecture. The helpless students are expected not only to listen but to take notes; then they are expected to memorize what we have said, with all our firstly's and secondly's and thirdly's; and finally they are expected to give it all back to us in the examination. Such a system—so the charge runs—stifles all originality and all life. Instead, the modern pedagogical expert comes with a message of hope; instead of memorizing facts, he says, true education consists in learning to think; drudgery is a thing of the past, and self-expression is to take its place.

In such a charge, there may be an element of truth; possibly there was a time in education when memory was over-estimated and thinking was deprived of its rights. But if the education of the past was one-sided in its emphasis upon acquaintance with facts, surely the pendulum has now swung to an opposite extreme which is more disastrous still. It is a travesty upon our pedagogic method when we are represented as regarding a mere storing up of lectures in the mind of the student as an end in itself. In point of fact, we regard it as a means to an end, but a very necessary means; we regard it not as a substitute for independent thinking, but as a necessary prerequisite for it. The student who accepts what we say without criticism and without thinking of his own is no doubt very unsatisfactory; but equally unsatisfactory is the student who undertakes to criticize what he knows nothing whatever about. Thinking cannot be carried on without the materials of thought; and the materials of thought are facts, or else assertions that are presented as facts. A mass of details stored up in the mind does not in itself make a thinker; but on the other hand thinking is absolutely impossible without that mass of details. And it is just this latter impossible operation of thinking without the materials of thought which is being advocated by modern pedagogy and is being put into practice only too well by modern students. In the presence of this tendency, we believe that facts and hard work ought again to be allowed to come to their rights: it is impossible to think with an empty mind.

If the growth of ignorance is lamentable in secular education, it is tenfold worse in the sphere of the Christian religion and in the sphere of the Bible. Bible classes today often avoid a study of the actual contents of the Bible as they would avoid pestilence or disease; to many persons in the Church the notion of getting the simple historical contents of the Bible straight in the mind is an entirely new idea.

When one is asked to preach at a church, the pastor sometimes asks the visiting preacher to conduct his Bible class, and sometimes he gives a hint as to how the class is ordinarily conducted. He makes it very practical, he says; he gives the class hints as to how to live during the following week. But when I for my part actually conduct such a class, I most emphatically do not give the members hints as to how to live during the following week. That is not because such hints are not useful, but because they are not all that is useful. It would be very sad if a Bible class did not get practical directions; but a class that gets nothing but practical directions is very poorly prepared for life. And so when I conduct the class I try to give them what they do not get on other occasions; I try to help them get straight in their minds the doctrinal and historical contents of the Christian religion.

The absence of doctrinal teaching and preaching is certainly one of the causes for the present lamentable ignorance in the Church. But a still more influential cause is found in the failure of the most important of all Christian educational institutions. The most important Christian educational institution is not the pulpit or the school, important as these institutions are; but it is the Christian family. And that institution has to a very large extent ceased to do its work. Where did those of us who have reached middle life really get our knowledge of the Bible? I suppose my experience is the same as that of a good many of us. I did not get my knowledge of the Bible from Sunday School or from any other school, but I got it on Sunday afternoons with my mother at home. And I will venture to say that although my mental ability was certainly of no extraordinary kind I had a better knowledge of the Bible at fourteen years of age than is possessed by many students in the theological Seminaries of the present day. Theological students come for the most part from Christian homes; indeed in very considerable proportion they are children of the manse. Yet when they have finished college and enter the theological Seminary many of them are quite ignorant of the simple contents of the English Bible.

The sad thing is that it is not chiefly the students' fault. These students, many of them, are sons of ministers; and by their deficiencies they reveal the fact that the ministers of the present day are not only substituting exhortation for instruction, ethics for theology, in their preaching; but are even neglecting the education of their own children. The lamentable fact is that the Christian home, as an educational institution, has largely ceased to function.

Certainly that fact serves to explain to a considerable extent the growth of ignorance in the Church. But the explanation itself requires an explanation; so far we have only succeeded in pushing the problem farther back. The ignorance of the Church is explained by the failure of the Christian family as an educational institution; but what in turn explains that failure? Why is it that Christian parents have neglected the instruction of their children; why is it that preaching has ceased to be educational and doctrinal; why is it that even Sunday Schools and Bible classes have come to consider solely applications of Christianity without studying the Christianity that is to be applied?[1] These questions take us into the very heart of the situation; the growth of ignorance in the Church, the growth of indifference with regard to the simple facts recorded in the Bible, all goes back to a great spiritual movement, really skeptical in its tendency, which has been going forward during the last one hundred years—a movement which appears not only in philosophers and theologians such as Kant and Schleiermacher and Ritschl, but also in a widespread attitude of plain men and women throughout the world. The depreciation of the intellect, with the exaltation in the place of it of the feelings or of the will, is, we think, a basic fact in modern life, which is rapidly leading to a condition in which men neither know anything nor care anything about the doctrinal content of the Christian religion, and in which there is in general a lamentable intellectual decline.

This intellectual decline is certainly not appearing exclu-

---

1. For a salutary insistence upon the fact that if we are to have applied Christianity, we must also have "a Christianity to apply," see Francis Shunk Downs, "Christianity and Today," in the *Princeton Theological Review*, xx, 1922, pp. 287-304.

sively among persons who are trying to be evangelical in their views about the Bible; but it is at least equally manifest among those who hold the opposing view. A striking feature of recent religious literature is the abandonment of scientific historical method even among those who regard themselves as in the van of scientific progress.

Scientific historical method in the interpretation of the Bible requires that the Biblical writers should be allowed to speak for themselves. A generation or so ago that feature of scientific method was exalted to the dignity of a principle, and was honored by a long name. It was called "grammatico-historical exegesis." The fundamental notion of it was that the modern student should distinguish sharply between what he would have said or what he would have liked to have the Biblical writer say, and what the writer actually did say. The latter question only was regarded as forming the subject-matter of exegesis.

This principle, in America at least, is rapidly being abandoned. It is not, indeed, being abandoned in theory; lip-service is still being paid to it. But it is being abandoned in fact. It is being abandoned by the most eminent scholars.

It is abandoned by Professor Goodspeed, for example, when in his translation of the New Testament he translates the Greek word meaning "justify," in important passages, by "make upright."[2] I confess that it is not without regret that I should see the doctrine of justification by faith, which is the foundation of evangelical liberty, thus removed from the New Testament; it is not without regret that I should abandon the whole of the Reformation and return with Professor Goodspeed to the merit-religion of the Middle Ages. But the point that I am now making is not that Professor Goodspeed's translation is

---

2. Goodspeed, *The New Testament: An American Translation*, 1923.

unfortunate because it involves—as it certainly does—religious retrogression, but because it involves an abandonment of historical method in exegesis. It may well be that this question how a sinful man may become right with God does not interest the modern translator; but every true historian must certainly admit that it did interest the Apostle Paul. And the translator of Paul must, if he be true to his trust, place the emphasis where Paul placed it, and not where the translator could have wished it placed.

What is true in the case of Paul is also true in the case of Jesus. Modern writers have abandoned the historical method of approach. They persist in confusing the question what they could have wished that Jesus had been with the question what Jesus actually was. In reading one of the most popular recent books on the subject of religion, I came upon the following amazing assertion. "Jesus," the author says, "concerned himself but little with the question of existence after death."[3] In the presence of such assertions any student of history may well stand aghast. It may be that we do not make much of the doctrine of a future life, but the question whether Jesus did so is not a matter of taste but an historical question, which can be answered only on the basis of an examination of the sources of historical information that we call the Gospels.

And the result of such examination is perfectly plain. As a matter of fact, not only the thought of heaven but also the thought of hell runs all through the teaching of Jesus. It appears in all four of the Gospels; it appears in the sources, supposed to underlie the Gospels, which have been reconstructed, rightly or wrongly, by modern criticism. It imparts to the ethical teaching its peculiar earnestness. It is not an element which can be removed by any critical process, but simply suffuses the whole

3. Ellwood, *The Reconstruction of Religion,* 1922, p.141.

of Jesus' teaching and Jesus' life. "And fear not them which kill the body, but are not able to kill the soul: but rather fear him which is able to destroy both soul and body in hell."[4] "It is better for thee to enter into life with one eye, rather than having two eyes to be cast into hell fire"[5]—these words are not an excrescence in Jesus' teaching but are quite at the centre of the whole.

At any rate, if you are going to remove the thought of a future life from the teaching of Jesus, if at this point you are going to reject the *prima facie* evidence, surely you should do so only by a critical grounding of your procedure. And my point is that that critical grounding is now thought to be quite unnecessary. Modern American writers simply attribute their own predilections to Jesus without, apparently, the slightest scrutiny of the facts.

As over against this anti-intellectual tendency in the modern world, it will be one chief purpose of the present little book to defend the primacy of the intellect, and in particular to try to break down the false and disastrous opposition which has been set up between knowledge and faith.

4. Matt. x:28.
5. Matt. xviii:9.

2

The Importance of
Christian Scholarship*

The Importance of Christian Scholarship for Evangelism

It seems to me, as I stand here before you today, that there is one blessing in these days of defection and unbelief which we have come to value as we never valued it before. That is the blessing of Christian fellowship in the presence of a hostile world, and in the presence of a visible Church which too often has departed from the Word of God. Today, during the three meetings of this League, in the portion of the meetings which has been allotted to me, I am to have the privilege of delivering three addresses on the subject, "The Importance of Christian Scholarship."

It is no doubt unfortunate that the person who speaks about this subject should have so limited an experimental acquaintance with the subject about which he is endeavouring to speak; but in these days of anti-intellectualism you may be willing to hear a word in defence of the intellect, even from one whose qualifications for speaking on that subject are so limited as mine.

There was a time when the raising of the question as to the importance of Christian scholarship might have seemed to be ridiculous; there was a time when a man who does so much

* Addresses given at Bible League Meetings in Caxton Hall, Westminster, London, June 17, 1932.

13

talking as a minister or a Sunday School teacher does, and as no doubt every Christian ought to do, in the propagation of the Faith to which he adheres, would have regarded it as a matter of course that he ought to know something about the subject of which he undertakes to talk.

But in recent years we have got far beyond all such elementary considerations as that; modern pedagogy has emancipated us, whether we be in the pulpit or in the professor's chair or in the pew, from anything so irksome as earnest labour in the acquisition of knowledge. It never seems to occur to many modern teachers that the primary business of the teacher is to study the subject that he is going to teach. Instead of studying the subject that he is going to teach, he studies "education"; a knowledge of the methodology of teaching takes the place of a knowledge of the particular branch of literature, history or science to which a man has devoted his life.

This substitution of methodology for content in the preparation of the teacher is based upon a particular view of what education is. It is based upon the view that education consists primarily, not in the imparting of information, but in a training of the faculties of the child; that the business of the teacher is not to teach, but to develop in the child a faculty which will enable the child to learn.

This child-centred notion of education seems to involve emancipation from a vast amount of drudgery. It used to be thought necessary to do some hard work at school. When a textbook was given to a class, it was expected that the contents of the textbook should be mastered. But now all that has been changed. Storing up facts in the mind was a long and painful process, and it is indeed comforting to know that we can now do without it. Away with all drudgery and all hard work! Self-expression has taken their place. A great pedagogic discovery has been made—the discovery that it is possible to think with a completely empty mind.

It cannot be said that the results of the discovery are impressive. This child-centred notion of education has resulted, particularly in America, where it has been most ruthlessly applied, in a boundless superficiality of which we Americans certainly have little reason to be proud; but it has probably not been confined to America by any means. I wonder when the reaction will come. I wonder when we shall have that revival of learning which we so much need, and which I verily believe might be, in the providence of God, as was the Renaissance of the fifteenth century, the precursor of a Reformation in the Church. When that revival of learning comes, we may be sure that it will sweep away the present absurd over-emphasis upon methodology in teaching at the expense of content. We shall never have a true revival of learning until teachers turn their attention away from the mere mental processes of the child, out into the marvellous richness and variety of the universe and of human life. Not teachers who have studied the methodology of teaching, but teachers who are on fire with a love of the subjects that they are going to teach are the real torch-bearers of intellectual advance.

Certainly the present view of education is, when it is applied to the work of the preacher and of the teacher in the Church, sceptical to the core. It is summed up in what is called "religious education." I wonder sometimes at the readiness with which Christian people—I do not mean Church-members, but real Bible-believing Christians—use that term; for the ordinary implications of the term are quite opposed to the Christian religion. The fundamental notion underlying the ordinary use of the term "religious education" is that the business of the teacher in the Church is not to impart knowledge of a fixed body of truth which God has revealed, but to train the religious faculty of the child. The religious faculty of the child, it is supposed, may be trained by the use of the most widely diverse doctrinal content; it may be trained in this generation, perhaps, by the thought of a personal God; but in another generation it may be trained equally well by the thought of an ideal humanity as the only God there is. Thus the search for objective and permanent truth is given up, and instead we have turned our attention to the religious faculties of man. In other words men have become interested today in religion because they have ceased to believe in God.

As over against such scepticism, the Bible, from Genesis to Revelation, presents a body of truth which God has revealed; and if we hold the biblical view, we shall regard it as our supreme function, as teachers and as preachers and as Christian parents and as simple Christians, to impart a knowledge of that body of truth. The Christian preacher, we shall hold, needs above all to know the thing that he is endeavouring to preach.

But if knowledge is necessary to preaching, it does seem probable that the fuller the knowledge is, the better the preacher will be able to do his work. Underlying preaching, in other words, is Christian scholarship; and it is in defence of Christian scholarship that I have thought it might be fitting to say a few words to you today.

Christian scholarship is necessary to the preacher, and to the man who in whatever way, in public or in private, endeavours to proclaim the gospel to his fellow-men, in at least three ways.

In the first place, it is necessary for evangelism. In saying so, I am perfectly well aware of the fact that I am putting myself squarely in conflict with a method of religious work which is widely prevalent at the present time. Knowledge, the advocates of that method seem to think, is quite unnecessary to faith; at the beginning a man may be a Fundamentalist or a Modernist, he may hold a Christian or an anti-Christian view of Christ. Never mind; he is to be received, quite apart from his opinions, on the basis of simple faith. Afterwards, indeed, he will, if he has really been converted, read his Bible and come to a more and more correct view of Christ and of the meaning of Christ's death. If he does not come to a more and more correct view, one may perhaps suspect that his conversion was not a real one after all. But at the beginning all that is thought to be unnecessary. All that a man has to believe in at the beginning is conversion: he is saved on the basis of simple faith; correct opinions about God and Christ come later.

With regard to this method, it may of course be said at once that the "simple faith" thus spoken of is not faith at all; or, rather, it is not faith in Christ. A man cannot trust a person whom he holds to be untrustworthy. Faith always contains an intellectual element. A very little knowledge is often sufficient if a man is to believe, but some knowledge there must be. So if a man is to trust Christ he must know something about Christ; he may know only a very little, but without some knowledge he could not believe at all.

What these advocates of a "simple faith" which involves no knowledge of Christ really mean by "simple faith" is faith, perhaps; but it is not faith in Christ. It is faith in the practitioners of the method; but it is not faith in Christ. To have faith in Christ one must have knowledge of Christ, however slight; and it is not a matter of indifference whether the opinions held about Christ are true or false.

But is this modern anti-intellectualistic view of faith in accordance with the New Testament? Does the New Testament offer a man salvation first, on the basis of a psychological process of conversion or surrender—falsely called faith—and then preach the gospel to him afterwards; or does the New

Testament preach the gospel to him first, set forth to him first the facts about Christ and the meaning of His death, and then ask him to accept the One thus presented in order that his soul may be saved?

That question can be answered very simply by an examination of the examples of conversion which the New Testament contains.

Three thousand were converted on the day of Pentecost. They were converted by Peter's sermon. What did Peter's sermon contain? Did it contain merely an account of Peter's own experience of salvation; did it consist solely in exhortation to the people to confess their sins? Not at all. What Peter did on the day of Pentecost was to set forth the facts about Jesus Christ —His life, His miracles, His death, His resurrection. It was on the basis of that setting forth of the facts about Christ that the three thousand believed, confessed their sins, and were saved.

Paul and Silas were in prison one night at Philippi. There was a miracle; the prisoners were released. The gaoler was impressed and said, "What must I do to be saved?" Paul and Silas said; "Believe on the Lord Jesus Christ, and thou shalt be saved." Did the gaoler believe then and there; was he saved without further delay? I think not. We are expressly told that Paul and Silas, after that, "spake unto him the word of the Lord." Then and not till then was he baptised, and I think we are plainly to understand that then and not till then was he saved.

Our Saviour sat one day by the well. He talked with a sinful woman, and laid His finger upon the sore spot in her life. "Thou hast had five husbands," He said; "and he whom thou now hast is not thy husband." The woman then apparently sought to evade the consideration of the sin in her own life by asking a theological question regarding the right place in which to worship God. What did Jesus do with her theological question? Did He brush it aside after the manner of modern religious workers? Did He say to the woman: "You are evading the real question; do not trouble yourself about theological matters, but let us return to the consideration of the sin in your life." Not at all. He answered that theological question with the utmost fulness as though the salvation of the woman's soul depended on her obtaining the right answer. In reply to that sinful woman, and to what modern religious workers would have regarded as an evasive question, Jesus engaged in some of the profoundest theological teaching in the whole New Testament. A right view of God, according to Jesus, is not something that comes merely after salvation, but it is something important for salvation.

The Apostle Paul in the First Epistle to the Thessalonians gives a precious summary of his missionary preaching. He does so by telling what it was to which the Thessalonians turned when they were saved. Was it a mere programme of life to which they turned? Was it a "simple faith," in the modern sense which divorces faith from knowledge and supposes that a man can have "simple faith" in a person of whom he knows nothing or about whom he holds opinions that make faith in him absurd? Not at all. In turning to Christ those Thessalonian Christians turned to a whole system of theology. "Ye turned to God from idols," says Paul, "to serve the living and true God; and to wait for His Son from heaven, whom He raised from the dead, even Jesus, which delivereth us from the wrath to come." "Ye turned to God from idols"—there is theology proper. "And to wait for His Son from heaven"—there is Christology. "Whom He raised from the dead"—there is the supernatural act of God in history. "Even Jesus"—there is the humanity of our Lord. "Which delivereth us from the wrath to come"— there is the Christian doctrine of sin and the Christian doctrine of the Cross of Christ.

So it is in the New Testament from beginning to end. The examples might be multiplied indefinitely. The New Testament gives not one bit of comfort to those who separate faith from knowledge, to those who hold the absurd view that a man can trust a person about whom he knows nothing. What many men despise today as "doctrine" the New Testament calls the gospel; and the New Testament treats it as the message upon which salvation depends.

But if that be so, if salvation depends upon the message in which Christ is offered as Saviour, it is obviously important that we should get the message straight. That is where Christian scholarship comes in. Christian scholarship is important in order that we may tell the story of Jesus and His love straight and full and plain.

At this point, indeed, an objection may arise. Is not the gospel a very simple thing, it may be asked; and will not its simplicity be obscured by too much scholarly research? The objection springs from a false view of what scholarship is; it springs from the notion that scholarship leads a man to be obscure. Exactly the reverse is the case. Ignorance is obscure; but scholarship brings order out of confusion, places things in their logical relations, and makes the message shine forth clear.

There are, indeed, evangelists who are not scholars, but scholarship is necessary to evangelism all the same. In the first place, though there are evangelists who are not scholars, the greatest evangelists, like the Apostle Paul and like Martin Luther, have been scholars. In the second place, the evangelists who are not scholars are dependent upon scholars to help them get their message straight; it is out of a great underlying fund of Christian learning that true evangelism springs.

That is something that the Church of our day needs to take to heart. Life, according to the New Testament, is founded upon truth; and the attempt to reverse the order results only in despair and in spiritual death. Let us not deceive ourselves, my friends.

Christian experience is necessary to evangelism; but evangelism does not consist merely in the rehearsal of what has happened in the evangelist's own soul. We shall, indeed, be but poor witnesses for Christ if we can tell only what Christ has done for the world or for the Church and cannot tell what He has done personally for us. But we shall also be poor witnesses if we recount only the experiences of our own lives. Christian evangelism does not consist merely in a man's going about the world saying: "Look at me, what a wonderful experience I have, how happy I am, what wonderful Christian virtues I exhibit; you can all be as good and as happy as I am if you will just make a complete surrender of your wills in obedience to what I say." That is what many religious workers seem to think that evangelism is. We can preach the gospel, they tell us, by our lives, and do not need to preach it by our words. But they are wrong. Men are not saved by the exhibition of our glorious Christian virtues; they are not saved by the contagion of our experiences. We cannot be the instruments of God in saving them if we preach to them thus only ourselves. Nay, we must preach to them the Lord Jesus Christ; for it is only through the gospel which sets Him forth that they can be saved.

If you want health for your souls, and if you want to be the instruments of bringing health to others, do not turn your gaze forever within, as though you could find Christ there. Nay, turn your gaze away from your own miserable experiences, away from your own sin, to the Lord Jesus Christ as He is offered to us in the gospel. "As Moses lifted up the serpent in the wilderness, even so must the Son of Man be lifted up." Only when we turn away from ourselves to that uplifted Saviour shall we have healing for our deadly hurt.

It is the same old story, my friends—the same old story of the natural man. Men are trying today, as they have always been trying, to save themselves—to save themselves by their own act of surrender, by the excellence of their own faith, by mystic experiences of their own lives. But it is all in vain. Not that way is peace with God to be obtained. It is to be obtained only in the old, old way—by attention to something that was done once for all long ago, and by acceptance of the living Saviour who there, once for all, brought redemption for our sin. Oh, that men would turn for salvation from their own experience to the Cross of Christ; oh, that they would turn from the phenomena of religion to the living God!

That that may be done, there is but one way. It is not found in a study of the psychology of religion; it is not found in "religious education"; it is not found in an analysis of one's own spiritual states. Oh, no. It is found only in the blessed written Word. There are the words of life. There God speaks. Let us attend to His voice. Let us above all things know the Word. Let us study it with all our minds, let us cherish it with all our hearts. Then let us try, very humbly, to bring it to the unsaved. Let us pray that God may honour not the messengers but the message, that despite our unworthiness He may make His Word upon our unworthy lips to be a message of life.

The Importance of Christian Scholarship for the Defense of the Faith

In speaking of Christian scholarship before the Bible League, I am somewhat in the position of bringing coals to Newcastle, but perhaps you will take what I am saying as being an expression of hearty agreement with that scholarly work which your League has been carrying on so successfully for many years. This morning we considered the importance of Christian scholarship for evangelism. The gospel message, we observed, is not brought to a man after salvation has already been received, but it is brought to him in order that salvation may be received; and the fuller and plainer the message is, so much the more effective is it for the saving of souls.

But Christian scholarship is also necessary, in the second place, for the defence of the faith, and to this aspect of the subject I invite your attention this afternoon. There are, indeed, those who tell us that no defence of the faith is necessary. "The Bible needs no defence," they say; "let us not be forever defending Christianity, but instead let us go forth joyously to propagate Christianity." But I have observed one curious fact—when men talk thus about propagating Christianity without defending it, the thing that they are propagating is pretty sure not to be Christianity at all. They are propagating an anti-intellectualistic, non-doctrinal Modernism; and the reason why it requires no defence is simply that it is so completely in accord with the current of the age. It causes no more disturbance than does a chip that floats downward with a stream. In order to be an adherent of it, a man does not need to resist anything at all; he needs only to drift, and automatically his Modernism will be of the most approved and popular kind. One thing needs always to be remembered in the Christian Church—true Christianity, now as always, is radically contrary to the natural man, and it cannot possibly be maintained without a constant struggle. A chip that floats downwards with the current is always at peace; but around every rock the waters foam and rage. Show me a professing Christian of whom all men speak well, and I will show you a man who is probably unfaithful to His Lord.

Certainly a Christianity that avoids argument is not the Christianity of the New Testament. The New Testament is full of argument in defence of the faith. The Epistles of Paul are full of argument—no one can doubt that. But even the words of Jesus are full of argument in defence of the truth of what Jesus was saying. "If ye then, being evil, know how to give good gifts unto your children, how much more shall your Father which is in heaven give good things to them that ask him?" Is not that a well-known form of reasoning, which the logicians would put in its proper category? Many of the parables of Jesus are argumentative in character. Even our Lord, who spoke in the plenitude of divine authority, did condescend to reason with men. Everywhere the New Testament meets objections fairly, and presents the gospel as a thoroughly reasonable thing.

Some years ago I was in a company of students who were discussing methods of Christian work. An older man, who had had much experience in working among students, arose and said that according to his experience you never win a man to Christ until you stop arguing with him. When he said that, I was not impressed.

It is perfectly true, of course, that argument alone is quite insufficient to make a man a Christian. You may argue with him from now until the end of the world; you may bring forth the most magnificent arguments: but all will be in vain unless there be one other thing—the mysterious, creative power of the Holy Spirit in the new birth. But because argument is insufficient, it does not follow that it is unnecessary. Sometimes it is used directly by the Holy Spirit to bring a man to Christ. But more frequently it is used indirectly. A man hears an answer to objections raised against the truth of the Christian religion; and at the time when he hears it he is not impressed. But afterwards, perhaps many years afterwards, his heart at last is touched: he is convicted of sin; he desires to be saved. Yet without that half-forgotten argument he could not believe; the gospel would not seem to him to be true, and he would remain in his sin. As it is, however, the thought of what he has heard long ago comes into his mind; Christian apologetics at last has its day; the way is open, and when he will believe he can believe because he has been made to see that believing is not an offence against truth.

Sometimes, when I have tried—very imperfectly, I confess —to present arguments in defence of the resurrection of our Lord or of the truth, at this point or that, of God's Word, someone has come up to me after the lecture and has said to me very kindly: "We liked it, and we are impressed with the considerations that you have adduced in defence of the faith; but, the trouble is, we all believed in the Bible already, and the persons that really needed the lecture are not here." When someone tells me that, I am not very greatly disturbed. True, I should have liked to have just as many sceptics as possible at my lecture; but if they are not there I do not necessarily think that my efforts are all in vain. What I am trying to do by my apologetic lecture is not merely—perhaps not even primarily— to convince people who are opposed to the Christian religion. Rather am I trying to give to Christian people—Christian parents or Sunday School teachers—materials that they can use, not in dealing with avowed sceptics, whose backs are up against Christianity, but in dealing with their own children or with the pupils in their classes, who love them, and long to be Christians as they are, but are troubled by the hostile voices on every side.

It is but a narrow view of Christian apologetics that regards the defence of the faith as being useful only in the immediate winning of those who are arguing vigorously on the other side. Rather is it useful most of all in producing an intellectual atmosphere in which the acceptance of the gospel will seem to be something other than an offence against truth. Charles Spurgeon and D.L. Moody, in the latter years of the nineteenth century, were facing a situation entirely different from that which faces the evangelists of today. They were facing a world in which many people in their youth had been imbued with Christian convictions, and in which public opinion, to a very considerable extent, was in favour of the Christian faith. Today, on the other hand, public opinion, even in England and America, is predominantly opposed to the Christian faith, and the people from their youth are imbued with the notion that Christian convictions are antiquated and absurd. Never was there a stronger call of God than there is today for a vigorous and scholarly defence of the faith.

I believe that the more thoughtful of the evangelists are coming to recognize that fact. There was a time, twenty-five or thirty years ago, when the evangelists regarded the work of Christian apologists as either impious or a waste of time. Here are souls to be saved, they said; and professors in theological seminaries insist on confusing their students' minds with a lot of German names, instead of preaching the simple gospel of Christ. But today a different temper often prevails. Evangelists, if they be real evangelists, real proclaimers of the unpopular message that the Bible contains, are coming more and more to see that they cannot do without those despised theological professors after all. It is useless to proclaim a gospel that people cannot hold to be true: no amount of emotional appeal can do anything against the truth. The question of fact cannot permanently be evaded. Did Christ or did He not rise from the dead; is the Bible trustworthy or is it false? In other words, the twelfth chapter of I Corinthians is coming again to its rights. We are coming to understand how many-sided is the work of Christ; the eye is ceasing to "say to the hand, 'I have no need of thee.' " Certainly one thing is clear—if Christian apologetics suffers, injury will come to every member of the body of Christ.

But if we are to have Christian apologetics, if we are to have a defence of the faith, what kind of defence of the faith should it be?

In the first place, it should be directed not only against the opponents outside the Church but also against the opponents within. The opponents of Holy Scripture do not become less dangerous, but they become far more dangerous, when they are within ecclesiastical walls.

At that point, I am well aware that widespread objection arises at the present time. Let us above all, men say, have no controversy in the Church; let us forget our small theological differences and all repeat together Paul's hymn to Christian love. As I listen to such pleas, my Christian friends, I think I can detect in them rather plainly the voice of Satan. That voice is heard, sometimes, on the lips of good and truly Christian men, as at Caesarea Philippi it was heard on the lips of the greatest of the Twelve. But Satan's voice it is, all the same.

Sometimes it comes to us in rather deceptive ways.

I remember, for example, what was said in my hearing on one occasion, by a man who is generally regarded as one of the leaders of the evangelical Christian Church. It was said at the climax of a day of devotional services. "If you go heresy-hunting for the sin in your own wicked hearts," said the speaker, as nearly as I can remember his words, "you will have no time for heresy-hunting for the heretics outside."

Thus did temptation come through the mouth of a well-meaning man. The "heretics," to use the term that was used by that speaker, are, with their helpers, the indifferentists, in control of the church within the bounds of which that utterance was made, the Presbyterian Church in the United States of America, as they are in control of nearly all the larger Protestant churches in the world. A man hardly need to "hunt" them very long if he is to oppose them. All that he needs to do is to be faithful to the Lord Jesus Christ, and his opposition to those men will follow soon enough.

But is it true, as this speaker seemed to imply, that there is a conflict between faithfulness to Christ in the ecclesiastical world and the cultivation of holiness in one's own inner life? My friends, it is not true, but false. A man cannot successfully go heresy-hunting against the sin in his own life if he is willing to deny His Lord in the presence of the enemies outside. The two battles are intimately connected. A man cannot fight success-fully in one unless he fights also in the other.

Again, we are told that our theological differences will disappear if we will just get down on our knees together in prayer. Well, I can only say about that kind of prayer, which is indifferent to the question whether the gospel is true or false, that it is not Christian prayer; it is bowing down in the house of Rimmon. God save us from it! Instead, may God lead us to the kind of prayer in which, recognizing the dreadful condition of the visible Church, recognizing the unbelief and the sin which dominate it today, we who are opposed to the current of the age both in the world and in the Church, facing the facts as they are, lay those facts before God, as Hezekiah laid before Him the threatening letter of the Assyrian enemy, and humbly ask Him to give the answer.

Again, men say that instead of engaging in controversy in the Church, we ought to pray to God for a revival; instead of polemics, we ought to have evangelism. Well, what kind of revival do you think that will be? What sort of evangelism is it that is indifferent to the question what evangel is it that is to be preached? Not a revival in the New Testament sense, not the evangelism that Paul meant when he said, "Woe is unto me, if I preach not the gospel." No, my friends, there can be no true evangelism which makes common cause with the enemies of the Cross of Christ. Souls will hardly be saved unless the evangelists can say with Paul: "If we or an angel from heaven preach any other gospel than that which we preached unto you, let him be accursed!" Every true revival is born in controversy, and leads to more controversy. That has been true ever since our Lord said that He came not to bring peace upon the earth but a sword. And do you know what I think will happen when God sends a new Reformation upon the Church? We cannot tell when that blessed day will come. But when the blessed day does come, I think we can say at least one result that it will bring. We shall hear nothing on that day about the evils of controversy in the Church. All that will be swept away as with a mighty flood. A man who is on fire with a message never talks in that wretched, feeble way, but proclaims the truth joyously and fearlessly, in the presence of every high thing that is lifted up against the gospel of Christ.

But men tell us that instead of engaging in controversy about doctrine we ought to seek the power of the living Holy Spirit. A few years ago we had in America, as I suppose you had here, a celebration of the anniversary of Pentecost. At that time, our Presbyterian Church was engaged in a conflict, the gist of which concerned the question of the truth of the Bible. Was the Church going to insist, or was it not going to insist, that its ministers should believe that the Bible is true? At that time of decision, and almost, it seemed, as though to evade the issue, many sermons were preached on the subject of the Holy Spirit. Do you think that those sermons, if they really were preached in that way, were approved by Him with whom they dealt? I fear not, my friends. A man can hardly receive the power of the Holy Spirit if he seeks to evade the question whether the blessed Book that the Spirit has given us is true or false.

Again, men tell us that our preaching should be positive and not negative, that we can preach the truth without attacking error. But if we follow that advice we shall have to close our Bible and desert its teachings. The New Testament is a polemic book almost from beginning to end. Some years ago I was in a company of teachers of the Bible in the colleges and other educational institutions of America. One of the most eminent theological professors in the country made an address. In it he admitted that there are unfortunate controversies about doctrine in the Epistles of Paul; but, said he in effect, the real essence of Paul's teaching is found in the hymn to Christian love in the thirteenth chapter of I Corinthians; and we can avoid controversy today, if we will only devote the chief attention to that inspiring hymn. In reply, I am bound to say that the example was singularly ill-chosen. That hymn to Christian love is in the midst of a great polemic passage; it would never have been written if Paul had been opposed to controversy with error in the Church. It was because his soul was stirred within him by a wrong use of the spiritual gifts that he was able to write that glorious hymn. So it is always in the Church. Every really great Christian utterance, it may almost be said, is born in controversy. It is when men have felt compelled to take a stand against error that they have risen to the really great heights in the celebration of truth.

But in defending the faith against the attack upon it that is being made both without and within the Church, what method of defence should be used?

In answer to that question, I have time only to say two things. In the first place, the defence, with the polemic that it involves, should be perfectly open and above board. I have just stated, that I believe in controversy. But in controversy I do try to observe the Golden Rule; I do try to do unto others as I would have others do unto me. And the kind of controversy that pleases me in an opponent is a controversy that is altogether frank.

Sometimes I go into a company of modern men. A man gets up upon the platform, looks out benignly upon the audience, and says: "I think, brethren, that we are all agreed about this"—and then proceeds to trample ruthlessly upon everything that is dearest to my heart. When he does that, I feel aggrieved. I do not feel aggrieved because he gives free expression to opinions that are different from mine. But I feel aggrieved because he calls me his "brother" and assumes, prior to investigation, that I agree with what he is going to say. A kind of controversy that pleases me better than that is a kind of controversy in which a man gets up upon the platform, looks out upon the audience, and says: "What is this? I see that one of those absurd Fundamentalists has somehow strayed into this company of educated men"—and then proceeds to call me by every opprobrious term that is to be found in one of the most unsavoury paragraphs of Roget's *Thesaurus*. When he does that, I do not feel too much distressed. I can even endure the application to me of the term "Fundamentalist," though for the life of me I cannot see why adherents of the Christian religion, which has been in the world for some nineteen hundred years, should suddenly be made an "-ism," and be called by some strange new name. The point is that that speaker at least does me the honour of recognizing that a profound difference separates my view from his. We understand each other perfectly, and it is quite possible that we may be, if not brothers (I object to the degradation of that word), yet at least good friends.

In the second place, the defence of the faith should be of a scholarly kind. Mere denunciation does not constitute an argument; and before a man can refute successfully an argument of an opponent, he must understand the argument that he is endeavouring to refute. Personalities, in such debate, should be kept in the background; and analysis of the motives of one's opponents has little place.

That principle, certainly in America, has been violated constantly by the advocates of the modernist or indifferentist position in the Church. It has been violated by them far more than by the defenders of God's Word. Yet the latter, strangely enough, have received the blame. The representatives of the dominant Modern-indifferentist forces have engaged in the most violent adjectival abuse of their opponents; yet they have been called sweet and beautiful and tolerant: the defenders of the Bible, and of the historic position of the Church have spoken courteously, though plainly, in opposition, and have been called "bitter" and "extreme." I am reminded of the way in which an intelligent American Indian is reported (I saw it in the American magazine *The Saturday Evening Post,* a few months ago) to have characterized the terminology used in histories of the wars between the white men and the men of his race. "When you won," said the Indian, "it was, according to your histories, a'battle'; when we won, it was a 'massacre.' "

Such, I suppose, is the treatment of the unpopular side in every conflict. Certainly it is the treatment which we receive today. Men have found it to be an effective way of making themselves popular, to abuse the representatives of so unpopular a cause as that which we Bible-believing Christians represent.

Yet I do not think we ought to be dismayed. If in these days of unbelief and defection in the Church we are called upon to bear just a little bit of the reproach of Christ, we ought to count ourselves honoured, and certainly we ought not to mitigate in the slightest measure the plainness either of our defence of the truth or of our warnings against error. Men's favour is worth very little after all, in comparison with the favour of Christ.

But certainly we should strive to keep ourselves free from that with which we are charged. Because our opponents are guilty, that is no reason why we should make ourselves guilty too.

It is no easy thing to defend the Christian faith against the mighty attack that is being brought against it at the present day. Knowledge of the truth is necessary, and also clear acquaintance with the forces hostile to the truth in modern thought.

At that point, a final objection may arise. Does it not

involve a terrible peril to men's souls to ask them—for example, in their preparation for the ministry—to acquaint themselves with things that are being said against the gospel of the Lord Jesus Christ? Would it not be safer to learn only of the truth, without acquainting ourselves with error? We answer, "Of course it would be *safer.*" It would be far safer, no doubt, to live in a fool's paradise and close one's eyes to what is going on in the world today, just as it is safer to remain in secure dugouts rather than to go over the top in some great attack. We save our souls, perhaps, by such tactics, but the Lord's enemies remain in possession of the field. It is a great battle indeed, this intellectual battle of today; deadly perils await every man who engages in that conflict; but it is the Lord's battle, and He is a great Captain in the fight.

There are, indeed, some perils that should be avoided— particularly the peril of acquainting ourselves with what is said against the Christian religion without ever obtaining any really orderly acquaintance with what can be said for it. That is the peril to which a candidate for the ministry, for example, subjects himself when he attends only one of the theological colleges where the professors are adherents of the dominant naturalistic view. What does such a course of study mean? It means simply this, that a man does not think the historic Christian faith, which has given him his spiritual nurture, to be worthy of a fair hearing. That is my only argument in advising a man to study, for example, at an institution like Westminster Theological Seminary, which I have the honour to serve. I am not asking him to close his eyes to what can be said against the historic faith. But, I am telling him that the logical order is to learn what a thing is before one attends exclusively to what can be said against it; and I am telling him further, that the way to learn what a thing is is not to listen first to its opponents, but to grant a full hearing to those who believe in it with all their minds and hearts. After that has been done, after our students, by pursuing the complete course of study, have obtained something like an orderly acquaintance with the marvelous system of truth that the Bible contains, then the more they listen to what can be said against it, the better defenders of it they will probably be.

Let us, therefore, pray that God will raise up for us today true defenders of the Christian faith. We are living in the midst of a mighty conflict against the Christian religion. The conflict is carried on with intellectual weapons. Whether we like it or not, there are millions upon millions of our fellow-men who reject Christianity for the simple reason that they do not believe Christianity to be true. What is to be done in such a situation?

We can learn, at this point, a lesson from the past history of the Church. This is not the first time during the past nineteen hundred years when intellectual objections have been raised against the gospel of Christ. How have those objections been treated? Have they been evaded, or have they been faced? The answer is writ large in the history of the Church. The objections have been faced. God has raised up, in time of need, not only evangelists to appeal to the multitudes, but also Christian scholars to meet the intellectual attack. So it will be in our day, my friends. The Christian religion flourishes not in the darkness but in the light. Intellectual slothfulness is but a quack remedy for unbelief; the true remedy is consecration of intellectual powers to the service of the Lord Jesus Christ.

Let us not fear for the result. Many times, in the course of the past nineteen hundred years, men have predicted that in a generation or so the old gospel would be forever forgotten. Yet the gospel has burst forth again, and set the world aflame. So it may be in our age, in God's good time and in His way. Sad indeed are the substitutes for the gospel of Christ. The Church has been beguiled into By-path Meadow, and is now groaning in the dungeon of Giant Despair. Happy is the man who can point out to such a Church the straight, high road that leads over hill and valley to the City of God.

The Importance of Christian Scholarship for the Building Up of the Church

We have been discussing today the uses of Christian scholarship. It is important, we showed this morning, for evangelism; it is important, in the second place, as we showed this afternoon, for the defence of the faith. But it has still another use. It is important, in the third place, for the building up of the Church.

At this point, as at the first two points, we have the New Testament on our side. At the beginning of the Church's life, as we are told in the Book of Acts, the Apostolic Church continued steadfastly, not only in fellowship and in breaking of bread and prayers, but also in the apostles' teaching. There is no encouragement whatever, in the New Testament, for the notion that when a man has been converted all has been done for him that needs to be done. Read the Epistles of Paul, in particular, from that point of view. Paul was the greatest of evangelists, and he gloried particularly in preaching the gospel just in places where it had never been heard; yet his Epistles are full of the edification or building up of those who have already been won; and the whole New Testament clearly discourages the exclusive nourishment of Christians with milk instead of with solid food.

In the modern Church, this important work of edification has been sadly neglected; it has been neglected even by some of those who believe that the Bible is the Word of God. Too often doctrinal preaching has been pushed from the primary place, in which it rightly belongs, to a secondary place; exhortation has taken the place of systematic instruction; and the people have not been built up. Is it any wonder that a Church thus nurtured is carried away with every wind of doctrine and is helpless in the presence of unbelief? A return to solid instruction in the pulpit, at the desk of the Sunday School teacher, and particularly in the home, is one of the crying needs of the hour.

I do not mean that a sermon should be a lecture; I do not mean that a preacher should address his congregation as a teacher addresses his class. No doubt some young preachers do err in that way. Impressed with the truth that we are trying to present tonight, they have endeavoured to instruct the people in Christian doctrine; but in their efforts to be instructive they have put entirely too many points into one sermon and the congregation has been confused. That error, unquestionably, should be avoided. But it should be avoided not by the abandonment of doctrinal preaching, but by our making doctrinal preaching real *preaching.* The preacher should present to his congregation the doctrine that the Holy Scripture contains; but he should fire the presentation of that doctrine with the devotion of the heart, and he should show how it can be made fruitful for Christian life.

One thing that impresses me about preaching today is the neglect of true edification even by evangelical preachers. What the preacher says is often good, and by it genuine Christian emotion is aroused. But a man could sit under that kind of preaching for a year or ten years and at the end of the time he would be just about where he was at the beginning. Such a lamentably small part of Scripture truth is used; the congregation is never made acquainted with the wonderful variety of what the Bible contains. I trust that God may raise up for us preachers of a different type; I trust that those preachers may not only build upon the one foundation which is Jesus Christ, but may build upon that foundation not wood, hay, stubble, but gold, silver, precious stones. Do you, if you are preachers or teachers in the Church, want to be saved merely so as through fire, or do you want your work to endure in the day of Jesus Christ? There is one work at least which I think we may hold, in all humility, to be sure to stand the test of judgment fire; it is the humble impartation, Sunday by Sunday, or day by day, of a solid knowledge not of what you say or what any man has said, but of what God has told us in His Word.

Is that work too lowly; is it too restricted to fire the ambition of our souls? Nay, my friends, a hundred lifetimes would not begin to explore the riches of what the Scriptures contain.

Some years ago, when I was still at Princeton Theological Seminary, before the reorganization of that institution, we received one of the countless questionnaires which in America have become, with one's neighbour's radio, one of the nuisances of modern life. The man who sent out the questionnaire was threatening, I believe, to write a book on theological education; and afterwards he carried out his threat. The questionnaire begged the question as many questionnaires do; it was not, if I remember rightly, in the slightest interested in the question whether a high scholarly standard was maintained in the study of the Bible; it did not seem to be much interested in discovering whether the students were or were not required to know the languages in which the Bible is written: but there were all sorts of questions about courses in hygiene and the like. In short, one prominent purpose of sending us the questionnaire seemed to be that of discovering whether Princeton Theological Seminary was or was not a medical school.

I am no longer connected with Princeton Theological Seminary, since its reorganization in 1929, and so cannot speak for that institution. But I may say that Westminster Theological Seminary, which I now have the honour to serve, is not pretending to be a medical school at all. We are not striving to train experts in hygiene or in first aid; we are not trying to make specialists in sociology or even specialists in religion. But what we are trying to do is to make specialists in the Bible and we think that that is a large enough specialty for any man to give to it his life.

What a world in itself the Bible is, my friends! Happy are those who in the providence of God can make the study of it very specifically the business of their lives; but happy also is every Christian who has it open before him and seeks by daily study to penetrate somewhat into the wonderful richness of what it contains.

A man does not need to read very long in the Bible before that richness begins to appear. It appears in the very first verse of the Bible; for the very first verse sets forth the being of God: "In the beginning God created the heaven and the earth."

We are told today, indeed, that that is metaphysics, and that it is a matter of indifference to the Christian man. To be a Christian, it is said, a man does not need at all to settle the question how the universe came into being. The doctrine of "fiat creation," we are told, belongs to philosophy, not to religion; and we can be worshippers of goodness even though goodness is not clothed with the vulgar trappings of power.

But to talk thus is to talk nonsense, for the simple reason that goodness divorced from power is a mere abstraction which can never call forth the devotion of a man's heart. Goodness inheres only in persons; goodness implies the power to act. Make God good only and not powerful, and you have done away not only with God, but with goodness as well.

Very different from such a pale abstraction, which identifies God with one aspect of the universe, is the God whom the first verse of Genesis presents. That God is the living God; it is He by whom the worlds were made and by whom they are upheld.

No, my friends, it is altogether wrong to say that the Christian religion can do perfectly well with many different types of philosophy, and that metaphysical questions are a matter of indifference to the Christian man. Nothing could be farther from the truth. As a matter of fact, everything else that the Bible contains is based upon the stupendous metaphysic that the first verse of Genesis contains. That was the metaphysic of our Lord Jesus Christ, and without it everything that He said and everything that He did would be vain. Underlying all His teaching and all His example is the stupendous recognition that God is the Maker and Ruler of the world; and the Bible from beginning to end depends upon that same "philosophy" of a personal God.

That philosophy ought to have been clear from an examination of the universe as it is; the Maker is revealed by the things that He has made. "The Heavens declare the glory of God, and the firmament sheweth his handy-work." "The invisible things of Him from the creation of the world are clearly seen, being understood by the things that are made, even His eternal power and Godhead." Natural religion has, therefore, the full sanction of the Bible; and at the foundation of every theological course should be philosophical apologetics, including the proof of the existence of a personal God, Creator and Ruler of the world.

I know there are those who tell us today that no such study is necessary; there are those who tell us that we should begin with Jesus, and that all we need to know is that God is like Jesus. They talk to us, in that sense, about the "Christlike God." But do you not see that if you relinquish the thought of a personal God, Creator and Ruler of the world, you are dishonouring the teaching of Jesus from beginning to end? Jesus saw in the lilies of the field the weaving of God; and the man who wipes out of his consciousness the whole wonderful revelation of God in nature, and then says that all that he needs to know is that God is like Jesus, is dishonouring at the very root of His teaching and of His example that same Jesus whom he is purporting to honour and serve.

The existence of a personal God should have been clear to us from the world as it is, but that revelation of God in nature has been obscured by sin, and to recover it and confirm it we need the blessed supernatural revelation that the Scriptures contain. How graciously that revelation is given! When we rise from the reading of the Bible, if we have read with understanding and with faith, what a wonderful knowledge we have of the living God!

In His presence, indeed, we can never lose the sense of wonder. Infinitesimal are the things that we know compared with the things that we do not know; a dreadful curtain veils the being of God from the eyes of man. Yet that curtain, in the infinite goodness of God, has been pulled gently aside, and we have been granted just a look beyond. Never can we cease to wonder in the presence of God; but enough knowledge has been granted to us that we may adore.

The second great mystery that the Bible presents is the mystery of man. And we are not allowed to wait long for that mystery. It is presented to us, as is the mystery of God, in the early part of the first book of the Bible. Man is there presented in his utter distinctness from the rest of creation; and then he is presented to us in the awful mystery of his sin.

At that point, it is interesting to observe how the Bible, unlike modern religious literature, always defines its terms; and at the beginning, when the Bible speaks of sin, it makes clear exactly what sin is. According to the Westminster Shorter Catechism, if you will pardon an allusion to that upon which your speaker was brought up, "sin is any want of conformity unto, or transgression of, the law of God." I do not remember, at the moment, what proof-texts the authors of the Westminster Standards used to support that definition. But they need hardly have looked further for such proof-texts than to the early part of Genesis. "Ye shall not eat of the tree," said God; man ate of the tree and died. Sin is there presented with the utmost clearness as the transgression of law. So it is presented in the whole of the Bible. Sin and law belong together. When we say "sin," we have said "law"; when we have said "law," then, man being what he now is, we have said "sin."

At the present time, the existence of law is being denied. Men no longer believe that there is such a thing as a law of God; and naturally they do not believe that there is such a thing as sin. Thoughtful men, who are not Christians, are aware of the problem that this stupendous change in human thinking presents to the modern world. Now that men no longer believe that there is a law of God, now that men no longer believe in obligatory morality, now that the moral law has been abandoned, what is to be put in its place, in order that an ordinarily decent human life may be preserved upon the earth? It cannot be said that the answers proposed for that question are as satisfactory as the way in which the question itself is put. It is impossible to keep back the raging seas of human passion with the flimsy mud embankments of an appeal either to self interest, or to what Walter Lippmann calls "disinterestedness." Those raging seas can only be checked by the solid masonry of the law of God.

Men are wondering today what is wrong with the world. They are conscious of the fact that they are standing over some terrible abyss. Awful ebullitions rise from that abyss. We have lost altogether the sense of the security of our Western civilisation. Men are wondering what is wrong.

It is perfectly clear what is wrong. The law of God has been torn up, as though it were a scrap of paper, and the inevitable result is appearing with ever greater clearness. When will the law be re-discovered? When it is re-discovered, that will be a day of terror for mankind: but it will also be a day of joy; for the law will be a schoolmaster unto Christ. Its terrors will drive men back to the little wicket gate, and to the way that leads to that place somewhat ascending where they will see the Cross.

Those are the two great presuppositions of everything else that the Bible contains; the two great presuppositions are the majesty of the transcendent God and the guilt and misery of man in his sin. But we are not left to wait long for the third of the great mysteries—the mystery of salvation. That too is presented at the beginning of Genesis, in the promise of a redemption to come.

The rest of the Bible is the unfolding of that promise. And when I think of that unfolding, when I try to take the Bible, not in part, but as a whole, when I contemplate not this doctrine or that, but the marvelous *system* of doctrine that the Bible contains, I am amazed that in the presence of such riches men can be content with that other gospel which now dominates the preaching of the Church.

When I think again of the wonderful metaphysic in the first verse of Genesis—"In the beginning God created the heaven and the earth"—when I think of the way in which throughout the Old Testament the majesty of that Creator God is presented with wonderful clearness, until the presentation culminates in the matchless fortieth chapter of Isaiah—"It is he that sitteth upon the circle of the earth, and the inhabitants thereof are as grasshoppers, that stretcheth out the heavens as a curtain, and spreadeth them out as a tent to dwell in"—when I think of the way in which in that same chapter the tenderness and the gentleness of that same awful God are presented, in a manner far beyond all human imagining—"He shall feed his flock like a shepherd: he shall gather the lambs with his arm, and carry them in his bosom, and shall gently lead those that are with young"—when I think of the wonderful gallery of portraits in the Old Testament, and compare it with the best efforts of men who have sought to penetrate into the secrets of human life and of the human heart; when I think of the gracious dealings of God with His people in Old Testament times, until the fulness of the time was come, and the Saviour was born into the world; when I think of the way in which His coming was accomplished, by a stupendous miracle indeed, but in wonderful quietness and lowliness; when I think of the songs of the heavenly host, and the way in which the infant Saviour was greeted in the Temple by those who had waited for the redemption of Jerusalem; when I stand in awe before that strange answer of the youthful Jesus, "Wist ye not that I must be about my Father's business?"; when I try to keep my imagination at rest, as Scripture bids me do, regarding those long, silent years at Nazareth; when I think of the day of His showing to Israel; when I think of the sternness of His teaching, the way in which He pulled the cloak from human sin, the way in which, by revealing through His words and His example the real demands of God, He took from mankind its last hope of any salvation to be obtained through its own goodness; when I think again, of the wonderful kindness of the Saviour; when I read how He forgave where none other would forgive, and helped where all other helpers had failed; when I think, above all, of that blessed thing which He did not only for men of long ago, who saw Him with their bodily eyes, but for every one of us if we be united with Him through faith, when He died in our stead upon the cross, and said in triumph, at the moment when His redeeming work was done, "It is finished"; when I enter into both the fear and the joy of those who found the tomb empty and saw the vision of angels which also said, "He is not here: for He is risen"; when I think of the way in which He was known to His disciples in the breaking of bread;

when I think of Pentecost and the pouring out of His Spirit upon the Church; when I attend to the wonderful way in which the Bible tells us how this Saviour may be our Saviour today, how you and I, sitting in this house tonight, can come into His presence, in even far more intimate fashion that that which was enjoyed by those who pushed their way unto Him as he sat amidst Scribes and Pharisees when He was on earth; when I think of the application of His redeeming work by the Holy Spirit:

"Be of sin the double cure,
Cleanse me from its guilt and power";

when I think of the glories of the Christian life, opened to us, not on the basis of human striving, but of that mighty act of God; when I read the last book of the Bible, and think of the unfolding of the glorious hope of that time when the once lowly Jesus, now seated on the throne of all being, shall come again with power —when I think of these things, I am impressed with the fact that the other gospel, which is dominant in the Church today, preached though it is by brilliant men, and admirable though it might have seemed if we had not compared it with something infinitely greater, is naught but "weak and beggarly elements," and that the humblest man who believes that the Bible is the Word of God is possessed of riches greater by far than all the learning of all the world and all the eloquence of all the preachers who now have the ear of an unfaithful Church.

3
Christianity and Culture*

One of the greatest of the problems that have agitated the Church is the problem of the relation between knowledge and piety, between culture and Christianity. This problem has appeared first of all in the presence of two tendencies in the Church—the scientific or academic tendency, and what may be called the practical tendency. Some men have devoted themselves chiefly to the task of forming right conceptions as to Christianity and its foundations. To them no fact, however trivial, has appeared worthy of neglect; by them truth has been cherished for its own sake, without immediate reference to practical consequences. Some, on the other hand, have emphasized the essential simplicity of the gospel. The world is lying in misery, we ourselves are sinners, men are perishing in sin every day. The gospel is the sole means of escape; let us preach it to the world while yet we may. So desperate is the need that we have no time to engage in vain babblings or old wives' fables. While we are discussing the exact location of the churches of Galatia, men are perishing under the curse of the law; while we are settling the date of Jesus' birth, the world is doing without its Christmas message.

---

* An address on "The Scientific Preparation of the Minister," delivered September 20, 1912, at the opening of the one hundred and first session of Princeton Theological Seminary, and in substance at a meeting of the Presbyterian Ministers' Association of Philadelphia, May 20, 1912. Reprinted from *The Princeton Theological Review,* Volume XI, 1913.

The representatives of both of these tendencies regard themselves as Christians, but too often there is little brotherly feeling between them. The Christian of academic tastes accuses his brother of undue emotionalism, of shallow argumentation, of cheap methods of work. On the other hand, your practical man is ever loud in his denunciation of academic indifference to the dire needs of humanity. The scholar is represented either as a dangerous disseminator of doubt, or else as a man whose faith is a faith without works. A man who investigates human sin and the grace of God by the aid solely of dusty volumes, carefully secluded in a warm and comfortable study, without a thought of the men who are perishing in misery every day!

But if the problem appears thus in the presence of different tendencies in the Church, it becomes yet far more insistent within the consciousness of the individual. If we are thoughtful, we must see that the desire to know and the desire to be saved are widely different. The scholar must apparently assume the attitude of an impartial observer—an attitude which seems absolutely impossible to the pious Christian laying hold upon Jesus as the only Saviour from the load of sin. If these two activities—on the one hand the acquisition of knowledge, and on the other the exercise and inculcation of simple faith—are both to be given a place in our lives, the question of their proper relationship cannot be ignored.

The problem is made for us the more difficult of solution because we are unprepared for it. Our whole system of school and college education is so constituted as to keep religion and culture as far apart as possible and ignore the question of the relationship between them. On five or six days in the week, we were engaged in the acquisition of knowledge. From this activity the study of religion was banished. We studied natural science without considering its bearing or lack of bearing upon natural theology or upon revelation. We studied Greek without opening the New Testament. We studied history with careful avoidance of that greatest of historical movements which was ushered in by the preaching of Jesus. In philosophy, the vital importance of the study for religion could not entirely be concealed, but it was kept as far as possible in the background. On Sundays, on the other hand, we had religious instruction that called for little exercise of the intellect. Careful preparation for Sunday-school lessons as for lessons in mathematics or Latin was unknown. Religion seemed to be something that had to do only with the emotions and the will, leaving the intellect to secular studies. What wonder that after such training we came to regard religion and culture as belonging to two entirely separate compartments of the soul, and their union as involving the destruction of both?

Upon entering the Seminary, we are suddenly introduced to an entirely different procedure. Religion is suddenly removed from its seclusion; the same methods of study are applied to it as were formerly reserved for natural science and for history. We study the Bible no longer solely with the desire to moral and spiritual improvement, but also in order to know. Perhaps the first impression is one of infinite loss. The scientific spirit seems to be replacing simple faith, the mere apprehension of dead facts to be replacing the practice of principles. The difficulty is perhaps not so much that we are brought face to face with new doubts as to the truth of Christianity. Rather is it the conflict of method, of spirit that troubles us. The scientific spirit seems to be incompatible with the old spirit of simple faith. In short, almost entirely unprepared, we are brought face to face with the problem of the relationship between knowledge and piety, or, otherwise expressed, between culture and Christianity.

The problem may be settled in one of three ways. In the first place, Christianity may be subordinated to culture. That solution really, though to some extent unconsciously, is being favored by a very large and influential portion of the Church today. For the elimination of the supernatural in Christianity— so tremendously common today—really makes Christianity merely natural. Christianity becomes a human product, a mere part of human culture. But as such it is something entirely different from the old Christianity that was based upon a direct revelation from God. Deprived thus of its note of authority, the gospel is no gospel any longer; it is a check for untold millions— but without the signature at the bottom. So in subordinating Christianity to culture we have really destroyed Christianity, and what continues to bear the old name is a counterfeit.

The second solution goes to the opposite extreme. In its effort to give religion a clear field, it seeks to destroy culture. This solution is better than the first. Instead of indulging in a shallow optimism or deification of humanity, it recognizes the profound evil of the world, and does not shrink from the most heroic remedy. The world is so evil that it cannot possibly produce the means for its own salvation. Salvation must be the gift of an entirely new life, coming directly from God. Therefore, it is argued, the culture of this world must be a matter at least of indifference to the Christian. Now in its extreme form this solution hardly requires refutation. If Christianity is really found to contradict that reason which is our only means of apprehending truth, then of course we must either modify or abandon Christianity. We cannot therefore be entirely independent of the achievements of the intellect. Furthermore, we cannot without inconsistency employ the printing-press, the railroad, the telegraph in the propagation of our gospel, and at the same time denounce as evil those activities of the human mind that produced these things. And in the production of these things not merely practical inventive genius had a part, but also, back of that, the investigations of pure science animated simply by the desire to know. In its extreme form, therefore, involving the abandonment of all intellectual activity, this second solution would be adopted by none of us. But very many pious men in the Church today are adopting this solution in essence and in spirit. They admit that the Christian must have a part in human culture. But they regard such activity as a necessary evil—a dangerous and unworthy task necessary to be gone through with under a stern sense of duty in order that thereby the higher ends of the gospel may be attained. Such men can never engage in the arts and sciences with anything like enthusiasm—such enthusiasm they would regard as disloyalty to the gospel. Such a position is really both illogical and unbiblical. God has given us certain powers of mind, and has implanted within us the ineradicable conviction that these powers were intended to be exercised. The Bible, too, contains poetry that exhibits no lack of enthusiasm, no lack of a keen appreciation of beauty. With this second solution of the problem we cannot rest content. Despite all we can do, the desire to know and the love of beauty cannot be entirely stifled, and we cannot permanently regard these desires as evil.

Are then Christianity and culture in a conflict that is to be settled only by the destruction of one or the other of the contending forces? A third solution, fortunately, is possible— namely consecration. Instead of destroying the arts and sciences or being indifferent to them, let us cultivate them with all the enthusiasm of the veriest humanist, but at the same time consecrate them to the service of our God. Instead of stifling the pleasures afforded by the acquisition of knowledge or by the appreciation of what is beautiful, let us accept these pleasures as the gifts of a heavenly Father. Instead of obliterating the distinction between the Kingdom and the world, or on the other hand withdrawing from the world into a sort of modernized intellectual monasticism, let us go forth joyfully, enthusiastically to make the world subject to God.

Certain obvious advantages are connected with such a solution of the problem. In the first place, a logical advantage. A man can believe only what he holds to be true. We are Christians because we hold Christianity to be true. But other men hold Christianity to be false. Who is right? That question can be settled only by an examination and comparison of the reasons adduced on both sides. It is true, one of the grounds for our belief is an inward experience that we cannot share—the great experience begun by conviction of sin and conversion and continued by communion with God—an experience which other men do not possess, and upon which, therefore, we cannot directly base an argument. But if our position is correct, we ought at least to be able to show the other man that *his* reasons *may* be inconclusive. And that involves careful study of both sides of the question. Furthermore, the field of Christianity is the world. The Christian cannot be satisfied so long as any human activity is either opposed to Christianity or out of all connection with Christianity. Christianity must pervade not merely all nations, but also all of human thought. The Christian, therefore, cannot be indifferent to any branch of earnest human endeavor. It must all be brought into *some* relation to the gospel. It must be studied either in order to be demonstrated as false, or else in order to be made useful in advancing the Kingdom of God. The Kingdom must be advanced not merely extensively, but also intensively. The Church must seek to conquer not merely every man for Christ, but also the whole of man. We are accustomed to encourage ourselves in our discouragements by the thought of the time when every knee shall bow and every tongue confess that Jesus is Lord. No less inspiring is the other aspect of that same great consummation. That will also be a time when doubts have disappeared, when every contradiction has been removed, when all of science converges to one great conviction, when all of art is devoted to one great end, when all of human thinking is permeated by the refining, ennobling influence of Jesus, when every thought has been brought into subjection to the obedience of Christ.

If to some of our practical men, these advantages of our solution of the problem seem to be intangible, we can point to the merely numerical advantage of intellectual and artistic activity within the Church. We are all agreed that at least one great function of the Church is the conversion of individual men. The missionary movement is the great religious movement of our day. Now it is perfectly true that men must be brought to Christ one by one. There are no labor-saving devices in evangelism. It is all hand-work. And yet it would be a great mistake to suppose that all men are equally well prepared to receive the gospel. It is true that the decisive thing is the regenerative power of God. That can overcome all lack of preparation, and the absence of that makes even the best preparation useless. But as a matter of fact God usually exerts that power in connection with certain prior conditions of the human mind, and it should be ours to create, so far as we can, with the help of God, those favorable conditions for the reception of the gospel. False ideas are the greatest obstacles to the reception of the gospel. We may preach with all the fervor of a reformer and yet succeed only in winning a straggler here and there, if we permit the whole collective thought of the nation or of the world to be controlled by ideas which, by the resistless force of logic, prevent Christianity from being regarded as anything more than a harmless delusion. Under such circumstances, what God desires us to do is to destroy the obstacle at its root. Many would have the seminaries combat error by attacking it as it is taught by its popular exponents. Instead of that they confuse their students with a lot of German names unknown outside the walls of the universities. That method of procedure is based simply upon a profound belief in the pervasiveness of ideas. What is today matter of academic speculation begins tomorrow to move armies and pull down empires. In that second stage, it has gone too far to be combatted; the time to stop it was when it was still a matter of impassionate debate. So as Christians we should try to mould the thought of the world in such a way as to make the acceptance of Christianity something more than a logical absurdity. Thoughtful men are wondering why the students of our great Eastern universities no longer enter the ministry or display any very vital interest in Christianity. Various totally inadequate explanations are proposed, such as the increasing attractiveness of other professions—an absurd explanation, by the way, since other professions are becoming so over-crowded that a man can barely make a living in them. The real difficulty amounts to this—that the thought of the day, as it makes itself most strongly felt in the universities, but from them spreads inevitably to the masses of the people, is profoundly opposed to Christianity, or at least—what is nearly as bad—it is out of all connection with Christianity. The Church is unable either to combat it or to assimilate it, because the Church simply does not understand it. Under such circumstances, what more pressing duty than for those who have received the mighty experience of regeneration, who, therefore, do not, like the world, neglect that whole series of vitally relevant facts which is embraced in Christian experience—what more pressing duty than for these men to make themselves masters of the thought of the world in order to make it an instrument of truth instead of error? The Church has no right to be so absorbed in helping the individual that she forgets the world.

There are two objections to our solution of the problem. If you bring culture and Christianity thus into close union—in the first place, will not Christianity destroy culture? Must not art and science be independent in order to flourish? We answer that it all depends upon the nature of their dependence. Subjection to any external authority or even to any human authority would be fatal to art and science. But subjection to God is entirely different. Dedication of human powers to God is found, as a matter of fact, not to destroy but to heighten them. God gave those powers. He understands them well enough not bunglingly to destroy His own gifts. In the second place, will not culture destroy Christianity? Is it not far easier to be an earnest Christian if you confine your attention to the Bible and do not risk being led astray by the thought of the world? We answer, of course it is *easier*. Shut yourself up in an intellectual monastery, do not disturb yourself with the thought of unregenerate men, and of course you will find it *easier* to be a Christian, just as it is easier to be a good soldier in comfortable winter quarters than it is on the field of battle. You save your own soul—but the Lord's enemies remain in possession of the field.

But by whom is this task of transforming the unwieldy, resisting the mass of human thought until it becomes subservient to the gospel—by whom is this task to be accomplished? To some extent, no doubt, by professors in theological seminaries and universities. But the ordinary minister of the gospel cannot shirk his responsibility. It is a great mistake to suppose that investigation can successfully be carried on by a few specialists whose work is of interest to nobody but themselves. Many men of many minds are needed. What we need first of all, especially, in our American churches, is a more general interest in the problems of theological science. Without that, the specialist is without the stimulating atmosphere which nerves him to do his work.

But no matter what his station in life, the scholar must be a regenerated man—he must yield to no one in the intensity and depth of his religious experience. We are well supplied in the world with excellent scholars who are without that qualification. They are doing useful work in detail, in Biblical philology, in exegesis, in Biblical theology, and in other branches of study. But they are not accomplishing the great task, they are not assimilating modern thought to Christianity, because they are without that experience of God's power in the soul which is of the essence of Christianity. They have only one side for the comparison. Modern thought they know, but Christianity is really foreign to them. It is just that great inward experience which it is the function of the true Christian scholar to bring into some sort of connection with the thought of the world.

During the last thirty years there has been a tremendous defection from the Christian Church. It is evidenced even by things that lie on the surface. For example, by the decline in church attendance and in Sabbath observance and in the number of candidates for the ministry. Special explanations, it is true, are sometimes given for these discouraging tendencies. But why should we deceive ourselves, why comfort ourselves by palliative explanations? Let us face the facts. The falling off in church attendance, the neglect of Sabbath observance—these things are simply surface indications of a decline in the power of Christianity. Christianity is exerting a far less powerful direct influence in the civilized world to-day than it was exerting thirty years ago.

What is the cause of this tremendous defection? For my part, I have little hesitation in saying that it lies chiefly in the intellectual sphere. Men do not accept Christianity because they can no longer be convinced that Christianity is true. It may be useful, but is it true? Other explanations, of course, are given. The modern defection from the Church is explained by the practical materialism of the age. Men are so much engrossed in making money that they have no time for spiritual things. That explanation has a certain range of validity. But its range is limited. It applies perhaps to the boom towns of the West, where men are intoxicated by sudden possibilities of boundless wealth. But the defection from Christianity is far broader than that. It is felt in the settled countries of Europe even more strongly than in America. It is felt among the poor just as strongly as among the rich. Finally it is felt most strongly of all in the universities, and that is only one indication more that the true cause of the defection is intellectual. To a very large extent, the students of our great Eastern universities—and still more the universities of Europe—are not Christians. And they are not Christians often just because they are students. The thought of the day, as it makes itself most strongly felt in the universities, is profoundly opposed to Christianity, or at least it is out of connection with Christianity. The chief obstacle to the Christian religion to-day lies in the sphere of the intellect.

That assertion must be guarded against two misconceptions. In the first place, I do not mean that most men reject Christianity consciously on account of intellectual difficulties. On the contrary, rejection of Christianity is due in the vast majority of cases simply to indifference. Only a few men have given the subject real attention. The vast majority of those who reject the gospel do so simply because they know nothing about it. But whence comes this indifference? It is due to the intellectual atmosphere in which men are living. The modern world is dominated by ideas which ignore the gospel. But it is out of all connection with it. It not only prevents the acceptance of Christianity. It prevents Christianity even from getting a hearing.

In the second place, I do not mean that the removal of intellectual objections will make a man a Christian. No conversion was ever wrought simply by argument. A change of heart is also necessary. And that can be wrought only by the immediate exercise of the power of God. But because intellectual labor is insufficient it does not follow, as is so often assumed, that it is unnecessary. God may, it is true, overcome all intellectual obstacles by an immediate exercise of His regenerative power. Sometimes He does. But He does so very seldom. Usually He exerts His power in connection with certain conditions of the human mind. Usually He does not bring into the Kingdom, entirely without preparation, those whose mind and fancy are completely dominated by ideas which make the acceptance of the gospel logically impossible.

Modern culture is a tremendous force. It affects all classes of society. It affects the ignorant as well as the learned. What is to be done about it? In the first place the Church may simply withdraw from the conflict. She may simply allow the mighty stream of modern thought to flow by unheeded and do her work merely in the back-eddies of the current. There are still some men in the world who have been unaffected by modern culture. They may still be won for Christ without intellectual labor. And they must be won. It is useful, it is necessary work. If the Church is satisfied with that alone, let her give up the scientific education of her ministry. Let her assume the truth of her message and learn simply how it may be applied in detail to modern industrial and social conditions. Let her give up the laborious study of Greek and Hebrew. Let her abandon the scientific study of history to the men of the world. In a day of increased scientific interest, let the Church go on becoming less scientific. In a day of increased specialization, of renewed interest in philology and in history, of more rigorous scientific method, let the Church go on abandoning her Bible to her enemies. They will study it scientifically, rest assured, if the Church does not. Let her substitute sociology altogether for Hebrew, practical expertness for the proof of her gospel. Let her shorten the preparation of her ministry, let her permit it to be interrupted yet more and more by premature practical activity. By doing so she will win a straggler here and there. But her winnings will be but temporary. The great current of modern culture will sooner or later engulf her puny eddy. God will save her somehow—out of the depths. But the labor of centuries will have been swept away. God grant that the Church may not resign herself to that. God grant she may face her problem squarely and bravely. That problem is not easy. It involves the very basis of her faith. Christianity is the proclamation of an historical fact—that Jesus Christ rose from the dead. Modern thought has no place for that proclamation. It prevents men even from listening to the message. Yet the culture of to-day cannot simply be rejected as a whole. It is not like the pagan culture of the first century. It is not wholly non-Christian. Much of it has been derived directly from the Bible. There are significant movements in it, going to waste, which might well be used for the defence of the gospel. The situation is complex. Easy wholesale measures are not in place. Discrimination, investigation is necessary. Some of modern thought must be refuted. The rest must be made subservient. But nothing in it can be ignored. He that is not with us is against us. Modern culture is a mighty force. It is either subservient to the gospel or else it is the deadliest enemy of the gospel. For making it subservient, religious emotion is not enough, intellectual labor is also necessary. And that labor is being neglected. The Church has turned to easier tasks. And now she is reaping the fruits of her indolence. Now she must battle for her life.

The situation is desperate. It might discourage us. But not if we are truly Christians. Not if we are living in vital communion with the risen Lord. If we are really convinced of the truth of our message, then we can proclaim it before a world of enemies, then the very difficulty of our task, the very scarcity of our allies becomes an inspiration, then we can even rejoice that God did not place us in an easy age, but in a time of doubt and perplexity and battle. Then, too, we shall not be afraid to call forth other soldiers into the conflict. Instead of making our theological seminaries merely centres of religious emotion, we shall make them battle-grounds of the faith, where, helped a little by the experience of Christian teachers, men are taught to fight their own battle, where they come to appreciate the real strength of the adversary and in the hard school of intellectual struggle learn to substitute for the unthinking faith of childhood the profound convictions of full-grown men. Let us not fear in this a loss of spiritual power. The Church is perishing to-day through the lack of thinking, not through an excess of it. She is winning victories in the sphere of material betterment. Such victories are glorious. God save us from the heartless crime of disparaging them. They are relieving the misery of men. But if they stand alone, I fear they are but temporary. The things which are seen are temporal; the things which are not seen are eternal. What will become of philanthropy if God be lost? Beneath the surface of life lies a world of spirit. Philosophers have attempted to explore it. Christianity has revealed its wonders to the simple soul. There lie the springs of the Church's power. But that spiritual realm cannot be entered without controversy. And now the Church is shrinking from the conflict. Driven from the spiritual realm by the current of modern thought, she is consoling herself with things about which there is no dispute. If she favors better housing for the poor, she need fear no contradiction. She will need all her courage, she will have enemies enough, God knows. But they will not fight her with argument. The twentieth century, in theory, is agreed on social betterment. But sin, and death, and salvation, and life, and God —about these things there is debate. You can avoid the debate if you choose. You need only drift with the current. Preach every Sunday during your Seminary course, devote the fag ends of your time to study and to thought, study about as you studied in college—and these questions will probably never trouble you. The great questions may easily be avoided. Many preachers are avoiding them. And many preachers are preaching to the air. The Church is waiting for men of another type. Men to fight her battles and solve her problems. The hope of finding them is the one great inspiration of a Seminary's life. They need not all be men of conspicuous attainments. But they must all be men of thought. They must fight hard against spiritual and intellectual indolence. Their thinking may be confined to narrow limits. But it must be their own. To them theology must be something more than a task. It must be a matter of inquiry. It must lead not to successful memorizing, but to genuine convictions.

The Church is puzzled by the world's indifference. She is trying to overcome it by adapting her message to the fashions of the day. But if, instead, before the conflict, she would descend into the secret place of meditation, if by the clear light of the gospel she would seek an answer not merely to the questions of the hour but, first of all, to the eternal problems of the spiritual world, then perhaps, by God's grace, through His good Spirit, in His good time, she might issue forth once more with power, and an age of doubt might be followed by the dawn of an era of faith.

4

Reforming the Government Schools*

At the root of the Christian attitude is a profound consciousness of the majesty of the moral law. But the majesty of the moral law is obscured in many ways at the present time, and most seriously of all in the sphere of education. Indeed, strangely enough, it is obscured in the sphere of education just by those who are becoming most keenly conscious of the moral bankruptcy of modern life. There is something radically wrong with our public education, it is said; an education that trains the mind without training the moral sense is a menace to civilization rather than a help; and something must quickly be done to check the impending moral collapse. To meet this need, various provisions are being made for moral training in our American public schools; various ethical codes are being formed for the instruction of children who are under the care of the State. But the sad thing is that these efforts are only making the situation tenfold worse; far from checking the ravages of immorality, they are for the most part themselves non-moral at the root. Sometimes they are also faulty in details, as when a recent moral code indulges in a veiled anti-Christian polemic by a reference to differences of "creed" that will no doubt be taken as belittling, and adopts the pagan notion of a human brotherhood already established, in distinction from the Christian notion of a brotherhood to be established by bringing men into common union with Christ. But the real objection to some, if not all, of these efforts does not depend upon details; it depends rather upon the fact that the basis of the effort is radically wrong. The radical error appears with particular clearness in a "Children's Morality Code" recently proposed by "The Character Education Institution" in Washington. That code contains eleven divisions, the sub-headings of which are as follows: I, "Good Americans Control Themselves"; II, "Good Americans Try to Gain and Keep Good Health"; III, "Good Americans are Kind"; IV, "Good Americans Play Fair"; V, "Good Americans are Self-Reliant"; VI, "Good Americans Do Their Duty"; VII, "Good Americans are Reliable"; VIII, "Good Americans are True"; IX, "Good Americans Try to do the Right Thing in the Right Way"; X, "Good Americans Work in Friendly Cooperation with Fellow-Workers"; XI, "Good Americans are Loyal."

Here we have morality regarded as a consequence of patriotism; the experience of the nation is regarded as the norm by which a morality code is to be formulated. This (thoroughly non-moral) principle appears in particularly crass form in "Point Two" of the Institution's *Five-Point Plan for Character Education in Elementary School Classrooms*: "The teacher," says the pamphlet, "presents the Children's Morality Code as a reliable statement of the conduct which is considered right among boys and girls who are loyal to Uncle Sam, and which is justified by the experience of multitudes of worthy citizens who have been Uncle Sam's boys and girls since the foundation of the nation. The teacher advises the children to study this Morality Code in order to find out what Uncle Sam thinks is right. . . ."

But what of those not infrequent cases where what "Uncle Sam" thinks is right is what God thinks is wrong? To say to a child, "Do not tell a lie because you are an American," is at bottom an immoral thing. The right thing to say is, "Do not tell a lie because it is wrong to tell a lie." And I do not think that it is an unconstitutional intrusion of religion into the public schools for a teacher to say that.

In general, the holier-than-thou attitude toward other peoples, which seems to be implied in the program of the Character Education Institution almost from beginning to end, is surely, at the present crisis in the history of the world, nothing short of appalling. The child ought indeed to be taught to love America, and to feel that whether it is good or bad it is *our* country. But the love of country is a very tender thing, and the best way to kill it is to attempt to inculcate it by force. And to teach, in defiance of the facts, that honesty and kindness and purity are peculiarly American virtues—this is surely harmful in the extreme. We blamed Germany, rightly or wrongly, for this kind of thing; yet now in the name of patriotism we advocate as truculent an inculcation of the same spirit as Prussia could ever have been accused of at its worst. Surely the only truly patriotic thing to teach the child is that there is one majestic moral law to which our own country and all the countries of the world are subject.

But the most serious fault of this program for "character building" is that it makes morality a product of experience, that it finds the norm of right conduct in the determination of that "which is justified by the experience of multitudes of worthy citizens who have been Uncle Sam's boys and girls since the foundation of the nation." That is wrong, as we have already observed, because it bases morality upon the experience of the nation; but it would also be wrong if it based it upon the experience of the whole human race. A code which is the mere result of human experimentation is not morality at all (despite the lowly etymological origin of our English word), but it is the negation of morality. And certainly it will not work. Moral standards were powerful only when they were invested with an unearthly glory and were treated as quite different in kind from all rules of expediency. The truth is that decency cannot be produced without principle. It is useless to try to keep back the raging sea of passion with the flimsy mud-embankments of an appeal to experience. Instead, there will have to be recourse again, despite the props afforded by the materialistic paternalism of the modern State, to the stern, solid masonry of the law of God. An authority which is man-made can never secure the reverence of man; society can endure only if it is founded upon the rock of God's commands.

It will not now be possible to propose in full our own solution of the difficult educational problem of which we have just been speaking. We have indeed such a solution. Most important of all, we think, is the encouragement of private schools and Church schools; a secularized public education, though perhaps necessary, is a necessary evil; the true hope of any people lies in a kind of education in which learning and piety go hand in hand. Christianity, we believe, is founded upon a body of facts; it is, therefore, a thing that must be taught; and it should be taught in Christian schools.

But taking the public school as an established institution, and as being, under present conditions, necessary, there are certain ways in which the danger of that institution may be diminished.

1. The function of the public school should be limited rather than increased. The present tendency to usurp parental authority should be checked.

2. The public school should pay attention to the limited, but highly important, function which it is now neglecting—namely, the impartation of knowledge.

3. The moral influence of the public-school teacher should be exerted in practical rather than in theoretical ways.

Certainly the (thoroughly destructive and immoral) grounding of morality in experience should be avoided. Unfortunately, the true grounding of morality in the will of God may, in our public schools, also have to be avoided. But if the teacher himself knows the absolute distinction between right and wrong, his personal influence, without theoretical grounding and without "morality codes," will appeal to the distinction between right and wrong which is implanted in the soul of the child, and the moral tone of the school will be maintained. We do not for a moment mean that that sort of training is sufficient; for the only true grounding of morality is found in the revealed will of God; but at least it will avoid doing harm.

4. The public-school system should be kept healthy by the absolutely free possibility of the competition of private schools and Church schools, and the State should refrain from such regulation of these schools as to make their freedom illusory.

5. Uniformity in education—the tendency which is manifested in the proposal of a Federal department of education in the United States—should be avoided as one of the very greatest calamities into which any nation can fall.

6. The reading of selected passages from the Bible, in which Jews and Catholics and Protestants and others can presumably agree, should not be encouraged, and still less should be required by law. The real centre of the Bible is redemption; and to create the impression that other things in the Bible contain any hope for humanity apart from that is to contradict the Bible at its root. Even the best of books, if it is presented in garbled form, may be made to say the exact opposite of what it means.

7. Public-school children should be released at certain convenient hours during the week, so that the parents, if they choose, may provided for their religious instruction; but the State should entirely refrain both from granting school credit

for work done in these hours and from exercising any control whatever either upon attendance or upon the character of the instruction.

Such are in general the alternative proposals that we might make if we were dealing with the problem which has led to the efforts at "character building" of which we have spoken. We recognize to the full the good motives of those who are making such efforts; but the efforts are vitiated by the false principle that morality is based upon experience; and so they will only serve, yet further, we fear, to undermine in the hearts of the people a sense of the majesty of the law of God.

5

The Necessity of the Christian School*

Two Reasons for the Christian School

The Christian school is to be favored for two reasons. In the first place, it is important for American liberty; in the second place, it is important for the propagation of the Christian religion. These two reasons are not equally important; indeed, the latter includes the former as it includes every other legitimate human interest. But I want to speak of these two reasons in turn.

In the first place, then, the Christian school is important for the maintenance of American liberty.

We are witnessing in our day a world-wide attack upon the fundamental principles of civil and religious freedom. In some countries, such as Italy, the attack has been blatant and unashamed; Mussolini despises democracy and does not mind saying so. A similar despotism now prevails in Germany; and in Russia freedom is being crushed out by what is perhaps the most complete and systematic tyranny that the world has ever seen.

But exactly the same tendency that is manifested in extreme form in those countries, is also being manifested, more slowly but none the less surely, in America. It has been given an enormous impetus first by the war and now by the economic

---

From *Forward in Faith*. Chicago: National Union of Christian Schools, 1934.

depression; but aside from these external stimuli it had its roots in a fundamental deterioration of the American people. Gradually the people has come to value principle less and creature comfort more; increasingly it has come to prefer prosperity to freedom; and even in the field of prosperity it cannot be said that the effect is satisfactory.

The result of this decadence in the American people is seen in the rapid growth of a centralized bureaucracy which is the thing against which the Constitution of the United States was most clearly intended to guard.

The Attack Upon Liberty

In the presence of this apparent collapse of free democracy, any descendant of the liberty-loving races of mankind may well stand dismayed; and to those liberty-loving races no doubt most of my hearers tonight belong. I am of the Anglo-Saxon race; many of you belong to a race whose part in the history of human freedom is if anything still more glorious; and as we all contemplate the struggle of our fathers in the winning of that freedom which their descendants seem now to be so willing to give up, we are impressed anew with the fact that it is far easier to destroy than to create. It took many centuries of struggle— much blood and many tears—to establish the fundamental principles of our civil and religious liberty; but one mad generation is sufficient to throw them all away.

It is true, the attack upon liberty is nothing new. Always there have been tyrants in the world; almost always tyranny has begun by being superficially beneficent, and always it has ended by being both superficially and radically cruel.

But while tyranny itself is nothing new, the technique of tyranny has been enormously improved in our day; the tyranny of the scientific expert is the most crushing tyranny of all. That tyranny is being exercised most effectively in the field of education. A monopolistic system of education controlled by the State is far more efficient in crushing our liberty than the cruder weapons of fire and sword. Against this monopoly of education by the State the Christian school brings a salutary protest; it contends for the right of parents to bring up their children in accordance with the dictates of their conscience and not in the manner prescribed by the State.

That right has been attacked in America in recent years in the most blatant possible ways. In Oregon, a law was actually passed some years ago requiring all children to attend the public schools—thus taking the children from the control of their parents and placing them under the despotic control of whatever superintendent of education might happen to be in office in the district in which they resided. In Nebraska, a law was passed forbidding the study of languages other than English, even in private schools, until the child was too old to learn them well. That was really a law making literary education a crime. In New York, one of the abominable Lusk Laws placed even private tutors under state supervision and control.

Temporary Relief

It is true that no one of these measures is in force at the present time. The Lusk Laws were repealed, largely through the efforts of Governor Alfred E. Smith. The Oregon School Law and the Nebraska Language Law were declared unconstitutional by the United States Supreme Court, and Justice McReynolds in the decision in the latter case gave expression to the great principle that in America the child is not the mere creature of the State.

Even such salutary decisions as that are not to be

contemplated with unmixed feelings by the lover of American institutions. They are based, I suppose, upon the great "Bill-of-Rights" provisions of the Constitution of the United States. But the original intent of those provisions was that they should be a check upon Congress, not that they should be a check upon the states. The fundamental rights of man were to be guaranteed, it was assumed, by the constitutions of the individual states, so far as the powers reserved to the states are concerned. It is a sign of appalling deterioration when the Federal Supreme Court steps in to do what the state courts ought to do. Nevertheless we cannot help rejoicing at the result. For the present at least, such an excess of tyranny as was put into effect in Oregon and has been seriously advocated in Michigan and other states is postponed.

Yet the forces inimical to liberty have not been discouraged by these temporary checks. They are at work with great persistency just at the present time, busying themselves particularly in the advocacy of two vicious measures, both of which concern childhood and youth.

The "Child Labor Amendment"

One of these is the mis-named "child-labor amendment" to the Constitution of the United States. That amendment masquerades under the cloak of humanitarianism; it is supposed to be intended to prevent sweat-shop conditions or the like. As a matter of fact, it is just about as heartless a piece of proposed legislation as could possibly be conceived. Many persons who glibly favor this amendment seem never to have read it for themselves. They have a vague notion that it merely gives power to Congress to enter right into your home and regulate or control or prevent altogether the helpful work of your children without which there can be no normal development of human character and no ordinary possibility of true happiness for mankind.

But, someone will say, Congress will never in the world be so foolish as that; the amendment does give Congress that power, but the power will never be exercised. Now, my friends, I will just say this: when I listen to an argument like that, I sometimes wonder whether the person who advances it can possibly be convinced by it himself. If these stupendous powers are never to be exercised, why should they be granted? The zeal for the granting of them, the refusal of the framers of the amendment to word the amendment in any reasonably guarded way, show plainly that the powers are intended to be exercised; and certainly they will be exercised, whatever the intention of the framers of the amendment may be. I will tell you exactly what will happen if this amendment is adopted by the states. Congress will pass legislation which, in accordance with the plain meaning of the language, will be quite unenforceable. The exact degree of enforcement will be left to Washington bureaus, and the individual family will be left to the arbitrary decision of officials. It would be difficult to imagine anything more hostile to the decency of family life and to all the traditions of our people. If there ever was a measure that looked as though it were made in Russia, it is this falsely so-called "child-labor amendment" to the Constitution of the United States. In reality, it can hardly be called an amendment to the Constitution. Rather is it the complete destruction of the Constitution; for if human life in its formative period—up to eighteen years in the life of every youth—is to be given to Federal bureaucrats, we do not see what else of very great value can remain. The old principles of individual liberty and local self-government will simply have been wiped out.

The Present Danger

This so-called child labor amendment was originally submitted to the states a number of years ago. It was in process of being rushed right through without any more examination than other amendments received. But then fortunately some patriotic citizens in Massachusetts, especially in the organization called "the Sentinels of the Republic," informed the people of the state what was really involved in this vicious measure. Massachusetts had a strict child labor law; it might have been expected, therefore, in accordance with the customary specious argument, to need protection against states where the child labor laws are less strict. Yet in a referendum the amendment was rejected by an overwhelming vote. Other states followed suit, and it looked as though this attack upon American institutions and the decencies of the American home had been repelled.

But we are living now in another period of hysteria, a period even worse than that which was found at the time of the war. So the so-called child labor amendment has been revived. State after state has adopted it, to a total number, I believe, of fourteen. It looks as though the enemies of American institutions might soon have their will, and as though the childhood and youth of our country might be turned over after all to the tender mercies of Washington bureaus. That disastrous result can only be prevented if there is an earnest effort of those who still think the preservation of the American home to be worthwhile.

Federal Intrusion

Another line of attack upon liberty has appeared in the advocacy of a Federal department of education. Repeatedly this vicious proposal has been introduced in Congress. It has been consistently favored by that powerful organization, the

National Education Association. Now without being familiar with the internal workings of that Association I venture to doubt whether its unfortunate political activities really represent in any adequate way the rank and file of its members or the rank and file of the public-school teachers of this country. When I appeared at a joint hearing before the Senate Committee on Education and Labor and the House Committee on Education in 1926, Mr. Lowrey of the House Committee asked me how it was that the resolution favoring the Federal department of education was passed unanimously by the National Education Association although he had discovered that many members of that Association were saying that they were opposed to it. Neither Mr. Lowrey nor I seemed to be able to give any very good explanation of this fact. At any rate, I desire to pay the warmest possible tribute to many thousands of conscientious men and women who are teachers in the public schools of this country. I do not believe that in the entire governmental aspect of education these teachers have any really effective representation.

The commission on the subject which President Hoover appointed, for example, was composed hardly at all of teachers, but almost exclusively of "educators." It had within its membership professors of "education," superintendents of schools and the like; but in the entire roll of its membership there was found, if I remember aright, hardly a single man eminent in any branch of literary studies or of natural science. The composition of that commission was typical of one of the fundamental vices in education in America at the present time—namely, the absurd over-emphasis upon methodology in the sphere of education at the expense of content. When a man fits himself in America to teach history or chemistry, it scarcely seems to occur to him, or rather it scarcely seems to occur to those who prescribe his studies for him, that he ought to study history or chemistry.

Instead, he studies merely "education." The study of education seems to be regarded as absolving a teacher from obtaining any knowledge of the subjects that he is undertaking to teach. And the pupils are being told, in effect, that the simple storing up in the mind of facts concerning the universe and human life is a drudgery from which they have now been emancipated; they are being told, in other words, that the great discovery has been made in modern times that it is possible to learn how to "think" with a completely empty mind. It cannot be said that the result is impressive. In fact the untrammeled operation of the effects of this great American pedagogic discovery is placing American schools far behind the schools of the rest of the civilized world.

The Evil of Uniformity

But that is perhaps something like a digression. Let us return to the "educators" and their general demand either for a Federal department of education or for Federal aid to the states. Such demands are in the interests of uniformity in the sphere of education. There should be, it is said, a powerful coordinating agency in education, to set up standards and encourage the production of something like a system. But what shall we say of such an aim? I have no hesitation, for my part, in saying that I am dead opposed to it. Uniformity in education, it seems to me, is one of the worst calamities into which any people can fall.

There are, it is true, some spheres in which uniformity is a good thing. It is a good thing, for example, in the making of Ford cars. In the making of a Ford car, uniformity is the great end of the activity. That end is, indeed, not always fully attained. Sometimes a Ford car possesses entirely too much individuality. My observation was, in the heroic days before the invention of self-starters, when a Ford was still a Ford, that sometimes a

Ford car would start and sometimes it would not start; and if it would not start there was no use whatever in giving it any encouraging advice. But although uniformity was not always perfectly attained, the aim, at least, was to attain it; the purpose of the whole activity was that one Ford car should be just as much like every other Ford car as it could possibly be made.

But what is good for a Ford car is not always good for a human being, for the simple reason that a Ford car is a machine while a human being is a person. Our modern pedagogic experts seem to deny the distinction, and that is one place where our quarrel with them comes in. When you are dealing with human beings, standardization is the last thing you ought to seek. Uniformity of education under one central governmental department would be a very great calamity indeed.

The Fallacy of "Equal Opportunity"

We are constantly told, it is true, that there ought to be an equal opportunity for all the children in the United States; therefore, it is said, Federal aid ought to be given to backward states. But what shall we say about this business of "equal opportunity?" I will tell you what I say about it; I am entirely opposed to it. One thing is perfectly clear—if all the children in the United States have equal opportunities, no child will have an opportunity that is worth very much. If parents cannot have the great incentive of providing high and special educational advantages for their own children, then we shall have in this country a drab and soul-killing uniformity, and there will be scarcely any opportunity for anyone to get out of the miserable rut.

The thing is really quite clear. Every lover of human freedom ought to oppose with all his might the giving of Federal aid to the schools of this country; for Federal aid in the long run inevitably means Federal control, and Federal control means control by a centralized and irresponsible bureaucracy, and control by such a bureaucracy means the death of everything that might make this country great.

Against this soul-killing collectivism in education, the Christian school, like the private school, stands as an emphatic protest. In doing so, it is no real enemy of the public schools. On the contrary, the only way in which a state-controlled school can be kept even relatively healthy is through the absolutely free possibility of competition by private schools and church schools; if it once becomes monopolistic, it is the most effective engine of tyranny and intellectual stagnation that has yet been devised.

The Propagation of the Faith

That is one reason why I favor the Christian school. I favor it in the interests of American liberty. But the other reason is vastly more important. I favor it, in the second place, because it is necessary to the propagation of the Christian Faith.

Thoughtful people, even many who are not Christians, have become impressed with the shortcomings of our secularized schools. We have provided technical education, which may make the youth of our country better able to make use of the advances of natural science; but natural science, with its command over the physical world is not all that there is in human life. There are also the moral interests of mankind; and without cultivation of these moral interests a technically trained man is only given more power to do harm. By this purely secular, non-moral and non-religious, training we produce not a real human being but a horrible Frankenstein, and we are beginning to shrink back from the product of our own hands.

The educational experts, in their conduct of their state-controlled schools, are trying to repair this defect and in doing so are seeking the cooperation of Christian people. I want to show you—and I do not think I shall have much difficulty in showing this particular audience—why such cooperation cannot be given.

"Character-Education"

In the first place, we find proposed to us today what is called "character-education" or "character-building." Character, we are told, is one thing about which men of all faiths are agreed. Let us, therefore, build character in common, as good citizens, and then welcome from the various religious faiths whatever additional aid they can severally bring. Let us first appeal to the children on a "civilization basis"—to use what I believe is the most recent terminology—and then let the various faiths appeal to whatever additional motives they may be able to adduce.

What surprises me about this program is not that its advocates propose it; for it is only too well in accord with the spirit of the age. But what really surprises me about it is that the advocates of it seem to think that a Christian can support it without ceasing at that point to be Christian.

In the first place, when this program of character-education is examined, it will be found, I think, to base character upon human experience; it will be found to represent maxims of conduct as being based upon the collective experience of the race. But how can they be based upon the collective experience of the race and at the same time, as the Christian must hold, be based upon the law of God. By this experiential morality the reverence for the law of God is being broken down. It cannot be said that the results—even judged by "civilization" standards (if I may borrow the terminology of my opponents for a moment)—is impressive. The raging tides of passion cannot successfully be kept back by the flimsy mud-embankments of an appeal to human experience. It is a feeble morality that can say nothing better for itself than that it works well.

Non-Christian Morality

For that reason, character-building, as practised in our public schools, may well prove to be character destruction. But suppose it were free from the defect that I have just mentioned. I do not see how it can possibly be free from it, if it remains, as it must necessarily remain, secular; but just suppose it were free from it. Just suppose we could have moral instruction in our public schools that should be based not upon human experience but upon something that might be conceived of as a law of God. Could a Christian consistently support even such a program as that?

We answer that question in the negative, but we do not want to answer it in the negative in any hasty way. It is perfectly true that the law of God is over all. There is not one law of God for the Christian and another law of God for the non-Christian. May not, therefore, the law be proclaimed to men of all faiths; and may it not, if it is so proclaimed, serve as a restraint against the most blatant forms of evil through the common grace of God; may it not even become a schoolmaster to bring men to Christ?

The answer is that if the law of God is proclaimed in public schools, to people of different faiths, it is bound, in the very nature of the case, to be proclaimed with optimism; and if it is proclaimed with optimism it is proclaimed in a way radically opposed to the Christian doctrine of sin. By hypothesis it is regarded as all that good citizens imperatively need to know; they may perhaps profitably know other things, but the fundamental notion is that if they know this they know all that is absolutely essential. But is not a law that is proclaimed to unredeemed persons with such optimism at best only an imperfect, garbled law? Is it not very different from the true and majestic law of God with its awful pronouncements of eternal death upon sinful man?

The answer to these questions is only too plain. A proclamation of morality which regards itself as all that is necessary—which regards itself as being capable at the most of non-essential supplementation by additional motives to be provided by Christianity or other faiths—is very different from that true proclamation of the law of God which may be a schoolmaster to bring men to Christ. It is not merely insufficient, but it is false; and I do not see how a consistent Christian can possibly regard it as providing any part of that nurture and admonition of the Lord which it is the duty of every Christian parent to give to his children.

Bible-Reading in Public Schools

What other solution, then, has the public school to offer for the problem which we are considering just now? Well, many people tell us that the reading of the Bible can be put into the public schools. Every educated man, we are told, ought to know something about the Bible; and no intelligent, broad-minded person, whether a Christian or not, ought to object to the bare reading of this great religious classic. So in many places we find the Bible being read in public schools. What shall we say about that?

For my part, I have no hesitation in saying that I am strongly opposed to it. I think I am just about as strongly opposed to the reading of the Bible in state-controlled schools as any atheist could be.

For one thing, the reading of the Bible is very difficult to separate from propaganda about the Bible. I remember, for example, a book of selections from the Bible for school reading, which was placed in my hands some time ago. Whether it is used now I do not know, but it is typical of what will inevitably occur if the Bible is read in public schools. Under the guise of being a book of selections for Bible-reading, it really presupposed the current naturalistic view of the Old Testament Scriptures.

But even where such errors are avoided, even where the Bible itself is read, and not in one of the current mistranslations but in the Authorized Version, the Bible still may be so read as to obscure and even contradict its true message. When, for example, the great and glorious promises of the Bible to the redeemed children of God are read as though they belonged of right to man as man, have we not an attack upon the very heart and core of the Bible's teaching? What could be more terrible, for example, from the Christian point of view, than the reading of the Lord's Prayer to non-Christian children, as though they could use it without becoming Christians, as though persons who have never been purchased by the blood of Christ could possibly say to God, "Our Father, which art in Heaven"? The truth is that a garbled Bible may be a falsified Bible; and when any hope is held out to lost humanity from the so-called ethical portions of the Bible apart from its great redemptive core, then the Bible is represented as saying the direct opposite of what it really says.

The Study of "Religion"

So I am opposed to the reading of the Bible in public schools. As for any presentation of general principles of what is called "religion," supposed to be exemplified in various positive religions, including Christianity, it is quite unnecessary for me to say in this company that such presentation is opposed to the Christian religion at its very heart. The relation between the Christian way of salvation and other ways is not a relation between the perfect and the imperfect, but it is a relation between the true and the false. The minute a professing Christian admits that he can find neutral ground with non-Christians in the study of "religion" in general, he has given up the battle, and has really, if he knows what he is doing, made common cause with that syncretism which is today, as it was in the first century of our era, the deadliest enemy of the Christian Faith.

What, then, should the Christian do in communities where there are no Christian schools? What policy should be advocated for the public schools?

I think there is no harm in advocating the release of public school children at convenient hours during the week for any religious instruction which their parents may provide. Even at this point, indeed, danger lurks at the door. If the State undertakes to exercise any control whatever over the use by the children of this time which is left vacant, even by way of barely requiring them to attend upon some kind of instruction in these hours, and still more clearly if it undertakes to give public-school credits for such religious instruction, then it violates fundamental principles and will inevitably in the long run seek to control the content of the instruction in the interests of the current syncretism. But if—as is, it must be admitted, very difficult—it can be kept free from these evils, then the arrangement of the public school schedule in such manner that convenient hours shall be left free for such religious instruction as the parents, entirely at their individual discretion, shall provide, is, I think, unobjectionable, and it may under certain circumstances be productive of some relative good.

The True Solution

But what miserable makeshifts all such measures, even at the best, are! Underlying them is the notion that religion embraces only one particular part of human life. Let the public schools take care of the rest of life—such seems to be the notion —and one or two hours during the week will be sufficient to fill the gap which they leave. But as a matter of fact the religion of the Christian man embraces the whole of his life. Without Christ he was dead in trespasses and sins, but he has now been made alive by the Spirit of God; he was formerly alien from the household of God, but has now been made a member of God's covenant people. Can this new relationship to God be regarded as concerning only one part, and apparently a small part, of his life? No, it concerns all his life; and everything that he does he should do now as a child of God.

It is this profound Christian permeation of every human activity, no matter how secular the world may regard it as being, which is brought about by the Christian school and the Christian school alone. I do not want to be guilty of exaggerations at this point. A Christian boy or girl can learn mathematics, for example, from a teacher who is not a Christian; and truth is truth however learned. But while truth is truth however learned, the bearing of truth, the meaning of truth, the purpose of truth, even in the sphere of mathematics, seem entirely different to the Christian from that which they seem to the non-Christian; and that is why a truly Christian education is possible only when Christian conviction underlies not a part, but all, of the curriculum of the school. True learning and true piety go hand in hand, and Christianity embraces the whole of life—those are great central convictions that underlie the Christian school.

I believe that the Christian school deserves to have a good

report from those who are without; I believe that even those of our fellow citizens who are not Christians may, if they really love human freedom and the noble traditions of our people, be induced to defend the Christian school against the assaults of its adversaries and to cherish it as a true bulwark of the State. But for Christian people its appeal is far deeper. I can see little consistency in a type of Christian activity which preaches the gospel on the street corners and at the ends of the earth, but neglects the children of the covenant by abandoning them to a cold and unbelieving secularism. If, indeed, the Christian school were in any sort of competition with the Christian family, if it were trying to do what the home ought to do, then I could never favor it. But one of its marked characteristics, in sharp distinction from the secular education of today, is that it exalts the family as a blessed divine institution and treats the scholars in its classes as children of the covenant to be brought up above all things in the nurture and admonition of the Lord.

Christian Heroism

I cannot bring this little address to a close without trying to pay some sort of tribute to you who have so wonderfully maintained the Christian schools. Some of you, no doubt, are serving as teachers on salaries necessarily small. What words can I possibly find to celebrate the heroism and unselfishness of such service? Others of you are maintaining the schools by your gifts, in the midst of many burdens and despite the present poverty and distress. When I think of such true Christian heroism as yours, I count everything that I ever tried to do in my life to be pitifully unworthy.

I can only say that I stand reverently in your presence as in the presence of brethren to whom God has given richly of His grace.

You deserve the gratitude of your country. In a time of spiritual and intellectual and political decadence, you have given us in America something that is truly healthy; you are to our country something like a precious salt that may check the ravages of decay. May that salt never lose its savor! May the distinctiveness of your Christian schools never be lost; may it never give place, by a false "Americanization," to a drab uniformity which is the most un-American thing that could possibly be conceived!

But if you deserve the gratitude of every American patriot, how much more do you deserve the gratitude of Christian men and women! You have set an example for the whole Christian world; you have done a thing which has elsewhere been neglected, and the neglect of which is everywhere in the Church! Above all, may our God richly bless you, and of His grace give you a reward with which all the rewards of earth are not for one moment worthy to be compared!

6

Shall We Have a Federal Department of Education?*

Mr. Chairman, Ladies and Gentlemen: I may say, if you will pardon a personal word, that the Chairman is incorrect in connecting me with Princeton University. As a matter of fact, I am connected with an institution which by some persons in certain fields is regarded as an opponent of liberty. But the charge is really very strange. I come, indeed, of a very strict sect, in company with my colleagues in the faculty of Princeton Theological Seminary; but I come of a sect that has always been devoted to the great principles of liberty. And to my mind one of the fundamental principles of liberty, which is involved in the present issue, is the principle of the right of voluntary association, the right of persons to associate themselves voluntarily for the propagation of their own views, however erroneous they may be thought to be by others, in the field of religion or in other spheres. You will find, I think, if you investigate the matter, that it is this principle of voluntary association which, strangely enough is being attacked by some persons in the name of liberty.

People seem to have a notion that a voluntary organization, religious or otherwise, is not free to exclude from the body of its official representatives those who hold principles which

---

* An address delivered before the Sentinels of the Republic, Washington, D.C. January 12, 1926. Reprinted from *The Woman Patriot*, February 15, 1926.

are diametrically opposed to its own. But as a matter of fact the principle of voluntary association, with maintenance of the purpose for which a voluntary association is formed, is at the very roots of human liberty.

But with that right of voluntary association goes insistence upon the most complete tolerance on the part of the State (which is an involuntary association) over against all other bodies, religious or social or whatever they may be, no matter how deleterious to the common welfare some men may think that they are.

It is time to come to the special subject upon which I have been asked to speak. Shall we have a Federal Department of Education?

One bill (S. 291-H.R. 5000) has been introduced in the present Congress which looks directly to the establishment of such a department. Another bill (H.R. 4097) not only provides for the establishment of such a department, but also provides in very radical form for the principle of Federal aid to the States, laying down even very definite conditions on which that aid may be received.

Another bill (S. 1334) has been introduced, and various proposals, as you know, have been made, looking to the reorganization of the Federal departments. What the ultimate relationship between these measures and the establishment of a Federal department will be, we cannot now tell; but I think that it is clear that just at the present juncture, in view of the very widespread support which the proposal has received, the question of a Federal Department of Education is very decidedly before the country.

Do we want a Federal Department of Education, or do we not? I think we do not. And I am asking your permission to tell you very briefly why.

We do not, I think, want a Federal Department of

Education because such a department is in the interests of a principle of uniformity or standardization in education which, if put into practice, would be the very worst calamity into which this country could fall.

This measure cannot be understood unless it be viewed in connection with related measures, like the so-called Child Labor Amendment; or like the Sterling-Reed bill with its predecessors and its successor, which provided for Federal aid to the States and which really would have taken away what measure of States' rights we possess.

People think very loosely in these days about receiving gifts. But on the basis of some observation of the reception of gifts in the educational field, I think I may give it as my opinion that a gift, in the educational field, always has a string tied to it. That may be observed with reference to various educational foundations. They provide ostensibly, sometimes, that the liberty of the institution to which they appropriate their funds is to be maintained. But in a very few years you will find that such institutions have become completely subservient to an outside board of control. And how much more obviously is that the case when we are dealing with the Federal Government, an agency which in every possible way is encroaching upon the power of the States. Federal aid in education inevitably means Federal control.

But the same result will be accomplished even by the measure that we now have directly in view. The establishment of a Federal Department of Education would be a step, and a decisive step, in exactly the same direction as those measures of which we have just been speaking.

We are indeed, sometimes actually asked to believe that a Federal Department of Education is a very innocent thing, that when it is established it will not do anything, and will not ask for any funds, except funds that are already provided for various

Federal agencies. But in this company I need not say that such modesty on the part of Federal departments is hardly in accordance with precedent. As a matter of fact it seems to be the fixed habit of every Federal bureau to ask for all the funds that it can get. I think that we may lay it down as a general principle that the more these bureaus get the more they want. And if we have a full-fledged Department of Education, with a Secretary at a salary of $15,000, and with hosts of other officers below that, we shall have a great Federal agency which is certain to embrace a larger and larger number of activities. And we shall have taken the really decisive step towards centralized control. It will be an extremely difficult, if not an absolutely impossible, thing to keep a Federal Department of Education as a merely paper affair and to prevent it from so extending its activities as to secure exactly the same results in the long run as the results there were aimed at by the so-called Child Labor Amendment and by the Sterling-Reed Bill.

It is clear therefore, that if we want to defeat this tendency in the educational field, now is the time to do it.

The reason why I am opposed to this proposal is that it represents a very ancient principle in the field of education, which, it seems to me, has been one of the chief enemies of human liberty for several thousand years—the principle, namely, that education is an affair essentially of the State, that education must be standardized for the welfare of the whole people and put under the control of government, that personal idiosyncrasies should be avoided. This principle of course, was enunciated in classic form in ancient Greece. It is the theory, for example, that underlies the *Republic* of Plato. But the principle was not only enunciated in theory; it was also, in some of the Greek states, put into practice. It is a very ancient thing—this notion that the children belong to the State, that their education must be provided for by the State in a way that makes for the

State's welfare. But that principle, I think you will find if you examine human history, is inimical at every step to liberty; and if there is any principle that is contrary to the whole genius of the Anglo-Saxon idea in government, it seems to me that it is in this principle of thoroughgoing State control in education.

Of course, we have a great many prophets of it today. I suppose it is the basic idea of Mr. H.G. Wells, in his popular *Outline of History.* The solution of the problem of the state, Mr. Wells believes, is in education; and by undertaking this problem in a more efficient way, possible because of increased ease of communication, the modern state can accomplish what the Roman Empire failed to accomplish.

I am willing to admit that in some fields standardization is an admirable thing. For example, standardization is an admirable thing in the making of Ford cars. But just because it is an admirable thing in the making of Ford cars it is a very harmful thing, I think, in the case of human beings. The reason is that a Ford car is a machine and a human being is a person. There are, indeed, a great many men in the modern world who deny the distinction. At this point we have an illustration of the utter falsity of the popular notion that philosophy has no practical effect upon the lives of the people, that it does not make any difference what a man believes in the sphere of ultimate reality. For the whole tendency that we are fighting today has underlying it a rather definite theory. Ultimately underlying it, I suppose, is the theory of the behaviorists—that the human race has at last found itself out, that it has succeeded in getting behind the scenes, that it has pulled off from human nature those tawdry trappings in which the actors formerly moved upon the human stage, that we have discovered that poetry and art and moral responsibility and freedom are delusions and that mechanism rules all. It is a mistake, we are told, to blame the criminal; the criminal is exactly what he is obliged to be, and good people are obliged to be exactly what they are. In other words, liberty is a delusion and human beings are just somewhat complicated machines.

It is probably not a thing which has come into the consciousness of very many people, but it is a fact all the same, that present-day education to a very large extent is dominated by exactly this theory, in one form or another. It is dominated partly by persons who hold the theory consciously; but it is dominated a great deal more by persons who have not the slightest notion what the ultimate source of their ideas in the field of education really is or what the result of them will be, but who are putting them into practice all the time.

What is the result of the application of this mechanistic theory in the sphere of education? I have no hesitation for my part in saying that the result is most lamentable. The result is simply intellectual as well as moral decline. It is obvious, I think, that there has been a moral decline; but what is not always observed is that there is also today a most astonishing and most lamentable intellectual decline. Poetry is silent; art is imitative or else bizarre; and if you examine the products of present-day education you will have to search far before you find a really well-stocked mind. I am not unaware, indeed, of the advantages of modern education; I am not unaware of the fact that a larger number of persons can read and write than formerly was the case. But despite all that I am still obliged to bring against the educational tendency of the present day in the sphere of public education the charge that the product is lamentably faulty. We are told, you know, that the old-fashioned notion of really learning things is out of date. Some time ago I heard one educator, a rather well-known man, tell a company of college professors that it is a great mistake to think that the business of the college professor is to teach the student anything; the real business of the college professor, he said, is to give the students an opportunity to learn; and what the student is in college to do is to "unify his world."

I am afraid that the students make a poor business of unifying their world—for the simple reason that they have no world to unify. They have not acquired a large enough number of facts even to practice the mental business of putting facts together; they are really being starved for want of facts. There has been an absurdly exaggerated emphasis on methodology at the expense of content in education; and the methodology that is actually advocated is based upon the false and vicious theory to which I have just referred—a false and vicious theory that destroys all the higher elements in human life.

With the persons who advocate this theory I cannot bring myself to agree. Somehow I cannot believe that the higher things in human life are delusions and that only the lower things are real. And therefore I do believe in freedom, and I do believe that persons are different from Ford cars.

What you want in a Ford car is just as little individuality as you can get. Sometimes, indeed—I may say that on the basis of my experience with a Ford car—sometimes you get entirely too much individuality. I soon learned by my own experience, before the days of self-starters, that sometimes a Ford will start and sometimes it won't, and that if it won't there is no use whatever in giving it any spiritual advice. Sometimes, in spite of what Mr. Ford can do, there has been an undue amount of individuality in the Ford car. But the *aim* of the whole activity at any rate, whatever the result may be, is to produce a thing that shall have just as little individuality as possible; the aim is that every Ford car shall be just as much like every other Ford car as it can possibly be made.

The aim of education, on the other hand, dealing, as education does, with human beings, is exactly the opposite; the aim of education is not to conform human beings to some fixed standard, but to preserve individuality, to keep human beings as much unlike one another in certain spheres as they possibly can be.

But that great aim of education, that personal, free, truly human aspect of education, can never have justice done to it under federal control. And that is the reason why the standardization of education that has already been carried on through the Federal Bureaus is deleterious. I have observed this in general: that when people talk about uniformity in education what they are really producing is not something that is uniformly high, but something that is uniformly low; they are producing a kind of education which reduces all to a dead level, which fails to understand the man who loves the high things that most of his fellowmen do not love. This degrading tendency is furthered I fear, by the present federal activities in education, and it will be given a stupendous impetus if this federal department is formed.

Just at this point, however, there may be an objection. I have been arguing, some men will tell me, against control of education by the State. But, it will be said, we already have control of education by the State, namely by the instrumentality of the individual States of our Union; and so—thus the objection runs—the authority of a Federal Department would not differ in principle from the authority which the State Governments already possess. I have been talking about individuality; I have said something about the rights of individual parents, by implication at least. "Well now," it will be said, "are not those rights already subject to the control of the individual States? But if they are, is not all that is being accomplished by this Federal measure merely the transference of this authority already possessed by Government to an agency that can exercise it in a wiser and more efficient way? Does not the principle, then, remain exactly the same?"

With regard to this objection, I am perfectly willing to admit that the State Governments have, in the sphere of education, in recent years committed some very terrible sins. We need think only, for example, of the Oregon school law, which sought to take children forcibly from their parents and place them under the despotic control of whatever superintendent of education happened to be in power in the district where the residence of the parents was found. Or we need only refer to the Nebraska language law (similar laws being enacted in a number of other States), which provided that no language other than English should be taught in any school, public or private, up to a certain grade—in point of fact until the children were too old ever to learn languages well. That was a law which actually made literary education a crime. Or we may think of that one of the two Lusk laws in the State of New York which provided that every teacher in all classes, public and private, formal and informal, should take out a State license and become subject to state visitation and control. These laws were blows, it seems to me, against the very vitals of liberty.

But the fate of all these measures is illustrative of the safeguards which we shall have if we keep this important concern of education under the control of the individual states. The Lusk laws were repealed. The Oregon school law and the Nebraska law fell before that last bulwark of our liberty, the United States Supreme Court. As Justice McReynolds said in the great decision in the Oregon school case, the child, in America, is not the mere creature of the state—a great principle which I think includes all that we are here endeavoring to maintain.

So it is to be observed that State measures—partly for reasons that have been brought out in what the previous speaker has said regarding the difficulty of securing a review of Congressional actions, and partly for other reasons—are very much more likely to be checked, if they are oppressive and against the spirit of our institutions, than are Federal measures.

Furthermore, there is a great safeguard in numbers. The beneficent fact is that there are forty-eight States in the Union. Some of them may become very bad in the sphere of education; but it is perhaps not likely that all of them will become utterly bad. Thus there is a great safeguard in the multiplicity of the States. For various reasons, then, I maintain that the principle is *not* the same when education is put under Federal control as when it is placed under State control.

Personally, indeed, I am opposed to certain tendencies in the sphere of public education in the States; I am opposed to the tendency by which the public school is made to do things that parents ought to do, such as providing moral instruction and the like. I am opposed to "morality codes" in the public schools. I have examined some of them and I think that they are vicious. They are not only faulty in detail, but they are wrong in principle. They base morality upon experience, instead of upon an absolute distinction between right and wrong. Despite the good motives of the compilers, therefore, they undermine the sense which children (and all the rest of us) ought to have of the majesty of the moral law.

That is, indeed, only a matter of personal opinion. I do not know whether it comes under the principles for which the Sentinels of the Republic stand. But you can take it for what it is worth. I, for my part, think that the functions of the public school ought to be diminished rather than broadened; and I believe that the public school ought to pay just a little bit of attention, perhaps, to that limited but not unimportant function which it is now almost wholly neglecting—namely, the impartation of knowledge.

Thus there are criticisms which I might make with regard

to public education in the individual States. But those criticisms do not fall directly under the subject with which we are dealing here, and I am not sure whether I can claim for them the authority of the Sentinels of the Republic. In these matters, I am giving voice to my own personal opinion. But perhaps I have said enough to show at least that as citizens we have important questions to decide when we are dealing with public education in the individual States.

At any rate, in the light of what I have just said, I do maintain that the danger is very much greater when education is placed under the control of the Federal Government, than the danger which undoubtedly does prevail even now on account of a mistaken use of State authority. Federal control of education, despite what is often said, most emphatically is not the same in principle as control by the States. And so I believe that this measure which would establish a Federal Department of Education ought to be defeated.

But I think that a great deal more than that ought to be done. I think that not only this particular measure ought to be defeated but the whole tendency that is represented by this measure ought to be defeated, the tendency towards a centralized standardization in education.

At this point, it is true, some persons hold up their hands in horror. "Do you mean to say," they ask us, "that we are actually going to continue to turn this important matter over to forty-eight separate and distinct states, to say nothing of the idiosyncrasies of individual parents, who want to send their children to all sorts of peculiar private schools and church schools? What utter confusion we shall have if we permit this sort of thing! Why, if we have this unlimited freedom of private schools and so on, we shall make a perfect mess of it."

Well, with regard to that, I may say that I think it is a good deal better to have confusion than it is to have death. For my part, I believe that in the sphere of education there ought to be the most unlimited competition—competition between one state and another and competition between state schools and private schools.

"But," it is said, "do you not believe in equal opportunity? Surely the Federal Government ought to help the States so that there will be equal opportunities for all the children in the whole country."

Now I am bound to say quite frankly, with regard to this matter of equal opportunity, that I am dead opposed to it. What ought you to do to a State that does not provide opportunities for its children equal to the opportunities that are provided by some other States? Ought you to tell the people of that State that it does not make any difference, because if they do not do the thing somebody else will do it for them? I think not. There ought to be unlimited competition in the sphere of education between one State and another State and between State schools and private schools. The State schools ought to be faced at every moment by the health-giving possibility of competition on the part of private schools and church schools. Only that will keep State education in a healthy way.

Of course, I understand perfectly well that competition in certain spheres has its disadvantages; and I am not going to talk about that. In some spheres it may have to be checked—we are not discussing that difficult question here. But when it comes to the sphere of the mind, I believe in absolutely unlimited competition. Anything else than that, it seems to me, will cause stagnation and death.

"But," people say, "how about efficiency?" Well, I think if the truth must be known, that that word "efficiency" is one of the most misused words in the language. Many persons seem to suppose that the mere use of that word constitutes an argument; they seem to suppose that you ought to regard it as a sufficient argument in favor of anything whatever when that thing is said to be efficient.

I notice also another word that is used in a somewhat similar way. It is the word "sincere." It often seems to be supposed that it is an argument in favor of a person who disagrees with us, when the fact is established that "he is perfectly sincere." It seems to be supposed that the fact that he is sincere constitutes a reason why I ought to agree with the person in question. But how absurd that is! As a matter of fact, the more sincere a man is in his advocacy of a thing that is wrong, the more opposed to him I am—not the more opposed to him in my estimate of his moral character (I may respect him personally because he is sincere), but the more opposed to the measures that he advocates. The more sincere he is in favor of something that I regard as bad, the more dangerous he is likely to be.

It is somewhat the same with regard to this matter of efficiency. Some men seem to think that it is admirable for its own sake. But surely efficiency involves doing something, and our attitude toward the efficiency all depends on whether the thing that is being done is good or bad.

A man does not admire efficiency very much when the efficiency is working to his disadvantage. You have all probably heard the story about the tramp that got up to the fourth floor of the department store. The floorwalker on the fourth floor kicked him down to the third floor; and there he fell afoul of the floorwalker on the third floor, who kicked him down to the second floor; and then the floorwalker on the second kicked him down to the ground floor; and then the floorwalker on the ground floor kicked him outside. He landed on his back outside, and when he got up he remarked in great admiration: "My, what a system!"

I am unable to attain quite that measure of complete

detachment that was attained by that tramp. Men want us to be overcome by admiration for a system that is working us harm. For my part, I flatly refuse. I am reminded of what Dr. Fabian Franklin said some years ago in an article in the *Yale Review*. Some persons, he said in effect, think that an objection to socialism is that it would not work. But so far as he was concerned, he said, his objection was rather that it might possibly work.

So it is with this Federal control of education. The better it works the worse it suits me; and if these people had their way— if everything could be reduced to a dead level, if everybody could be made like everybody else, if everybody came to agree with everybody else because nobody would be doing any thinking at all for himself, if all could be reduced to this harmony—do you think that the world would be a good place under those circumstances? No, my friends. It would be a drab, miserable world, with creature comforts in it and nothing else, with men reduced to the level of the beasts, with all the higher elements of human life destroyed.

Thus I am in favor of efficiency if it is directed to a good end; but I am not in favor of efficiency if it is directed to something that is bad.

As a matter of fact, Federal departments are not efficient, but probably the most inefficient things on the face of this planet. But if they were the most efficient agencies that history has ever seen, I should, in this field of education, be dead opposed to them. Efficiency in a good cause is good; but I am opposed to Federal efficiency in this sphere because the result of it is a thing that I regard as bad—namely, slavery. And I am not inclined to do what a great many people do today; I am not inclined to write "freedom" in quotation marks as though it were a sort of joke. I believe, on the contrary, that it is something that is very real. An ounce of freedom is worth a pound of efficiency. I think, too, that we may discern within the last year just the beginning of the rise of the love of liberty again in our people. I hope therefore that this measure may be defeated, and that all measures may be defeated that look in the same direction, and that we may return to the principle of freedom for individual parents in the education of their children in accordance with their conscience, and to the principle of freedom for the States, and to the reliance upon the multiplicity of them for a preservation of those things that have made our country great.

It is to be hoped that the indications of a returning love of liberty which are just beginning to appear are not illusory, but that America, despite opposition, is going to return to the freedom that used to be the very atmosphere that she breathed. But let us be perfectly clear about one thing—if liberty is not maintained with regard to education, there is no use trying to maintain it in any other sphere. If you give the bureaucrats the children, you might just as well give them everything else. That is the reason why I think that every one of us ought to be opposed with all his might and main to the sinister legislative measure that we have been considering today. No, we do *not* want a Federal Department of Education; and we do not want, in any form whatever, the slavery that a Federal Department of Education would bring.

7

Proposed Department of Education*

THURSDAY, FEBRUARY 25, 1926

CONGRESS OF THE UNITED STATES
SENATE COMMITTEE ON EDUCATION AND LABOR,
HOUSE COMMITTEE ON EDUCATION.

Washington, D.C.

The committee met, pursuant to adjournment, at 10 o'clock a.m., Senator Lawrence C. Phipps presiding.

Present: Senators Phipps (chairman), Ferris, Copeland, and Brookhart, of the Senate Committee, and Messrs. Reed of New York, Robison, Holaday, Lowrey, Black of New York, and Fletcher, of the House Committee.

Senator Phipps. The committee will be in order. We will hear first from Dr. J. Gresham Machen, of Princeton Theological Seminary.

Doctor Machen. Mr. Chairman and gentlemen of the Committee, there are two reasons why a man may be opposed to a bill which is introduced in Congress. One reason is that he thinks it will not accomplish its purpose. The other reason is that he thinks that the purpose that it is intended to accomplish is an evil purpose.

---

* Testimony before the House and Senate Committees, February 25, 1926.

It is for the latter reason that I am opposed to the bill which forms the subject of this hearing. The purpose of the bill is made explicit in the revised form of it which has been offered by Senator Means, in which it is expressly said that the department of public education, with the assistance of the advisory board to be created, shall attempt to develop a more uniform and efficient system of public common school education. The department of education, according to that bill, is to promote uniformity in education. That uniformity in education under central control it seems to me is the worst fate into which any country can fall. That purpose I think is implicit also in the other form of the bill, and it is because that is the very purpose of the bill that I am opposed to it.

This bill, I think, cannot be understood unless it is taken in connection with certain other measures of similar kind which have been proposed in the last few years; in the first place, of course, the so-called child-labor amendment to the Constitution of the United States, which I think was one of the most cruel and heartless measures that have ever been proposed in the name of philanthropy, which is saying a good deal. Another similar measure, of course, is the bill which has now been introduced, I believe, and which has appeared a number of times during the last few years, establishing in a very radical way a system of Federal aid to the States, with conditions on which this aid is to be received. It is perfectly clear of course, that if any such principle of Federal aid in education is established, the individual liberty of the States is gone, because I think we can lay it down as a general rule, with which everyone who has examined the course of education recently will agree, that money given for education, no matter what people say, always has a string tied to it. That appears in gifts of money by private foundations, and it appears far more, of course, when the gift comes from the Federal Government, which has already been encroaching to such an extent upon the powers of the States. But this bill establishing a Federal department of education, which has in it the principle of Federal aid, is a step and a very decisive step in exactly the same direction, and it is for that reason that we think it is to be opposed.

It is to be opposed, we think, because it represents a tendency which is no new thing, but has been in the world for at least 2,300 years, which seems to be opposed to the whole principle of liberty for which our country stands. It is the notion that education is an affair essentially of the State; that the children of the State must be educated for the benefit of the State; that idiosyncrasies should be avoided, and the State should devise that method of education which will best promote the welfare of the State.

That principle was put in classic form in ancient Greece in the *Republic* of Plato. It was put into operation, with very disastrous results in some of the Greek States. It has been in the world ever since as the chief enemy of human liberty. It appears in the world to-day. There are many apostles of it, such as Mr. H.G. Wells, for example. I suppose the root of his popular *Outline of History* is that with our modern methods of communication we can accomplish what the Roman Empire could not accomplish, because we can place education under the control of the State, and, avoiding such nonsense as literary education and the study of the classics, etc., can produce a strong unified state by having the State take up the business of education.

The same principle, of course, appears in practice in other countries in modern times, at its highest development in Germany, in disastrous form in Soviet Russia. It is the same idea. To that idea our notion has been diametrically opposed, and if you read the history of our race I think you will discover that our notion has been that parents have a right to educate children as they please; that idiosyncrasies should not be avoided; that the

State should prevent one group from tyrannizing over another, and that education is essentially not a matter of the State at all.

The principle of this bill, and the principle of all the advocates of it, is that standardization in education is a good thing. I do not think a person can read the literature of advocates of measures of this sort without seeing that that is taken almost without argument as a matter of course, that standardization in education is a good thing. Now, I am perfectly ready to admit that standardization in some spheres is a good thing. It is a good thing in the making of Ford cars; but just because it is a good thing in the making of Ford cars it is a bad thing in the making of human beings, for the reason that a Ford car is a machine and a human being is a person. But a great many educators today deny the distinction between the two, and that is the gist of the whole matter. The persons to whom I refer are those who hold the theory that the human race has now got behind the scenes, that it has got at the secrets of human behavior, that it has pulled off the trappings with which human actors formerly moved upon the scene of life, and has discovered that art and poetry and beauty and morality are delusions, and that mechanism really rules all. I think it is very interesting to observe how widespread that theory is in the education of the present day.

Sometimes the theory is held consciously. But the theory is much more operative because it is being put into operation by people who have not the slightest notion of what the ultimate source of its introduction into the sphere of education is. In this sphere we find an absolute refutation of the notion that philosophy has no effect upon life. On the contrary, a false philosophy, a false view of what life is, is made operative in the world today in the sphere of education through great hosts of teachers who have not the slightest notion of what the ultimate meaning is of the methods that they are putting into effect all the time.

For my part, I cannot bring myself to think, with these persons, that the lower things in human life are the only things that remain, and that all the higher things are delusions; and so I do not adhere to this theory. And for that reason I do not believe that we ought to adopt this principle of standardization in education, which is writ so large in this bill; because standardization, it seems to me, destroys the personal character of human life.

The aim in the making of Ford cars is to make every one just as much like every other one as possible; but the aim in education is to make human beings just as much unlike one another as possible. I admit that the aim in the case of Ford cars is not always attained very well. The removal of idiosyncrasies in Ford cars is not always perfectly carried out. I can say from my experience with Ford cars before the days of self-starters that sometimes a Ford car will start and sometimes it will not start, and if it will not start there is no use giving it any spiritual advice at all. Sometimes, despite everything that Mr. Ford can do, there is too much individuality in a Ford car; but the *purpose* is to make every one just as much like every other one as possible. That is the purpose of a great many educators when it comes to education to-day, and it is the purpose that underlies the tendency in this bill. It is to remove idiosyncrasies, to interfere with people who have peculiar ideas in education, and to try to produce a uniformity of education in this country.

I do not believe that the personal, free, individual character of education can be preserved when you have a Federal department laying down standards of education which become more or less mandatory to the whole country. Of course, there are people who say that a Federal department does not mean anything. They say that when they talk to men of our way of thinking. A good many people seem to have the notion that a Federal department, like the House of Lords during the Napoleonic wars, will "do nothing in particular and do it very well"; but for my part I do not believe, when you get a department with a secretary who has a salary of $15,000 and a great many secretaries under him, and when you get this dignity of a department, that you are going to find that that department is going to be very modest about the funds for which it asks.

I think it is perfectly plain that we are embarking on a policy here which cannot be reversed when it is once embarked upon. It is very much easier to prevent the formation of some agency that may be thought to be unfortunate than it is to destroy it after it is once formed. Now, I think, is the decisive time to settle this question whether we want the principle for which this department will stand.

But at that point, of course, there may be an objection. People will say: "Why, you have been arguing for individual liberty in education, and the right of individual parents to educate their children as they please, and all that; but is not that interfered with already by the States, and is not this bill the same in principle as the control of education by the individual States which we already have?" I am perfectly ready to admit that there have been grievous sins in the sphere of education on the part of individual States. We need only think of the Oregon school law, which actually attempted to take children forcibly from their parents and put them under the despotic control of whatever superintendent of education happened to be in power in the district where the parents resided. We need think only of the Nebraska language law, which was similar to laws in other States, which actually prevented, even in private schools, the study of languages until the children are at an age when every teacher knows they are too old ever to learn language well. It actually, therefore, made literary education—which most certainly is not overdone in this country—a crime. Finally we need only think of the Lusk laws of the State of New York, one of which actually provided that every teacher in a course of instruction, public or private, formal or informal, should take out a State license and be subject to State visitation and control.

I am perfectly ready to admit that no interference with liberty could possibly be more complete than measures such as those; but the fate of those measures is very instructive for the question with which we are dealing. The Lusk laws were repealed. The Oregon school law and the Nebraska language law fell before that last bulwark of our liberties, the United States Supreme Court, which may God protect; and Justice McReynolds said, in the Oregon school case, that the child is not the mere creature of the State. And in that principle there lies everything for which we are contending to-day.

Then in the States there is a great safeguard in numbers. There are 48 States at this time, and they are very different. So although it is perfectly conceivable that one State may go very bad, it is not, perhaps, likely that all of them will go utterly bad. There is great safety in numbers; and therefore I hold that the control of education by the Federal Government is very different in principle from the control that is already exercised by the States, because the control by the States can be checked better in a constitutional way than control by the Federal Government, and also because there is a great difference in principle between having control by one central authority and control by a great many different sources of authority.

But it will be said: "Why, do you actually mean that we should have these 48 States, each with its own separate system of education, and a lot of crazy private schools and church schools?" Why, people tell us we shall make a perfect mess of it if we have any such education as that. Well, I say, with respect to that, that I hope with all my might that we may go on making a mess of it. I had a great deal rather have confusion in the sphere of education than intellectual and spiritual death; and out of that "mess," as they call it—we call it liberty—there has come every fine thing that we have in our race to-day.

But then people say: "What is going to become of the matter of equal opportunity? Here you have some States providing inferior opportunities to others, and the principle of equal opportunity demands Federal aid." I may say, Mr. Chairman, with regard to this matter of equal opportunity, that I am dead opposed to it—dead opposed to the principle of equal opportunity. What shall be done with a State that provides opportunity for its children inferior to that provided by other States? Should the people of that State be told that it makes absolutely no difference, that Washington will do it if the State does not do it? I think not. I think we are encouraging an entirely false attitude of mind on the part of individual parents and on the part of individual States if we say that it makes no difference how responsibilities are met.

I believe that in the sphere of the mind we should have absolutely unlimited competition. There are certain spheres where competition may have to be checked, but not when it comes to the sphere of the mind; and it seems to me that we ought to have this state of affairs: That every State should be faced by the unlimited competition in this sphere of other States; that each one should try to provide the best for its children that it possibly can; and, above all, that all public education should be kept healthy at every moment by the absolutely free competition of private schools and church schools.

A public education that is faced by such competition is a beneficent result of modern life; but a public education that is not faced by such competition of private schools is one of the deadliest enemies to liberty that has ever been devised.

Unlimited competition, I think, should be the rule. We already have interchange of ideas in this country. We do not need what George Washington wanted, a national university, because we have both the ends that he desired to accomplish by a national university. You need only to look at the list of students in any of our great institutions in order to see that they come from all over this country. There is that interchange of ideas of which he spoke. And we have also universities in this country that do not make it necessary for anyone to go to Europe to get an education, as he said. If we had no universities, we might want a national agency in education, but we have universities, and we do not want to spoil the agencies that we already have— as the erection of a Federal department would check and spoil them in very many ways.

But then people say: "You know that this Federal department of education is in the interest of efficiency." They are always flinging that word "efficiency" at us as though when that word is spoken all argument at once is checked. Well, of course, "efficiency" just means doing things, and I think the important thing to know is whether the things that are being done are good or bad. If the things that are being done by any agency are good, I am in favor of efficiency; but if the things that are being done by the agency are bad, the less efficiency it has the better it suits me.

I think probably most of us have heard the story of the tramp who got up to the third floor of the department store. The floorwalker on the third floor kicked him down to the second floor, where he fell afoul of the floorwalker on the second floor, who kicked him down to the floorwalker on the first floor, and the floorwalker on the first floor kicked him out on the sidewalk. He landed on his back, and got up and said in a tone of deep admiration, "My! What a system." [Laughter.] Now, I am unable to develop the complete detachment or objectivity which was developed by that tramp. I am unable to admire efficiency when it is directed to an end which works harm to me; and the end of the efficiency of a Federal department of education would be the worst kind of slavery that could possibly be devised—a slavery in the sphere of the mind.

Of course, too, I might argue that Federal bureaus, when they have become overgrown, as they are now, are hardly very efficient agencies. In fact, I am inclined to think that they are the most inefficient agencies that can be found anywhere on the face of the planet. They are discouraging activities by other agencies which would perform the work a great deal better, even where harm is not done, as it is in this sphere, by the existence of the agency itself.

But even if Federal bureaus were the most efficient agencies that history has even seen, I should still be opposed all the more to this Federal department of education, because the result that it is aiming to accomplish is a thing that I hold to be bad, namely, slavery.

A great many educators, I think, have this notion that it is important to be doing something, to be going somewhere. They are interested in progress, and they do not seem to care very much in what direction the progress is being made. It is like a man who goes into the Union Station here, where all the trains start out the same way, and he gets through the gate somehow and sees a train that looks beautiful; it has a lovely observation car on it, and he gets on. When I do that, my ticket reads to Princeton. I get on this lovely train, and when it gets out of the station after half an hour the conductor comes through the train and looks at my ticket, and says: "Your ticket reads to Princeton, N.J., and we are bound for the West, and our first stop is Cumberland." I say: "Well, that makes no difference to me. This is a perfectly lovely train, and I am so glad to be on it; and which way is the dining car?"—and I just stay on it, and do not care where I am going.

That is exactly the way, it seems to me, with these people who, in the sphere of education, feel that if you call a thing a department of education, and try to spend money for education as you are spending it for battleships, somehow that is an advantage. It depends on the direction in which you are moving.

So that I find in this bill a decisive step in a direction where the progress, if persisted in, will lead to disaster; and what I am hoping for is not merely that this bill may be defeated, but that this whole tendency, gentlemen, may be checked. I think that is the important thing.

Mr. Robison. What do you refer to when you say "the whole tendency"?

Doctor Machen. The whole tendency toward uniformity in the sphere of education, and the whole principle of a central control as over against individual responsibility.

Mr. Robison. Do you object, then, to the activities of the Federal Government in the way of Federal aid to roads and to agriculture and to commerce and to labor?

Doctor Machen. I object in general to the principle of Federal aid; yes, sir.

Mr. Robison. I mean, to the activities of the Federal Government in agriculture and roads and commerce and labor?

Doctor Machen. I do in general. Of course, a line has to be drawn. The Federal Government has a right to regulate interstate commerce. There are certain powers that are delegated to it definitely by the Constitution, and I do not desire to speak about other subjects; but in general I am opposed, sir, to the principle of Federal aid in the spheres where the States are really in control.

Mr. Robison. In agriculture the activities of the Federal Government may have no relation to interstate commerce, but be directed to other matters.

Doctor Machen. I am opposed, sir, to the extension of the operation of the principle of Federal aid. I think that it has clearly gone too far even in other spheres; that it has clearly gone too far, and that it should be checked. But I do not desire to speak about other spheres. I am talking specifically about the sphere of education, and in that sphere the principle of limitation of competition, etc., as I have tried to explain, does not come in. In that sphere, I think, we should absolutely avoid the principle of Federal aid.

Senator Phipps. Doctor Machen, you are connected with the Princeton Theological Seminary. That is denominational; is it?

Doctor Machen. Yes, sir.

Senator Phipps. Which denomination is it?

Doctor Machen. It belongs to the Presbyterian church.

Senator Phipps. Reverting to your illustration of the Ford car, what has been the result of the plan adopted by the English schools for boys, such as Eaton and Rugby? Does it turn out boys all of the same type, all of the same mold, or does the system take away from their individuality?

Doctor Machen. I am not prepared to speak about the English public-school system, sir, because I do not know enough about it. I am not prepared to say how far it is monopolistic. I am prepared to say that I think that any central activities in Great Britain are no precedent whatever for central activities in this country. I believe with all my soul in the principle for this country of the division of power between the States and the Federal Government; and it is a very different matter, I think, when you deal with a country such as Great Britain. I do feel, sir, that it is plain that in Great Britain there is very great danger, because of present economic pressure, of the destruction of all of those principles of individual liberty which have made Great Britain great. They have the terrible evils of the present time; and it seems to me that in this country, where we have not the economic pressure, it is for us for the moment, where necessity is not upon us, to go straight on the road of individual freedom; not to be in a panic or turned aside from it.

Senator Phipps. Are there any further questions to be put to the witness?

Mr. Lowrey. I should like to ask some questions, Mr. Chairman. Doctor, are you a member of the National Education Association that is meeting here?

Doctor Machen. No, sir.

Mr. Lowrey. Were you at the meeting when the resolution was passed in favor of this bill?

Doctor Machen. No, sir; I was not. I have only read about it in the newspapers.

Mr. Lowrey. The question I intended to ask is about a matter that has puzzled me somewhat. It seems that the resolution was passed unanimously, and now I am finding a great many who are saying, "I am opposed to it, but I did not vote against it." I think not less than 8 or 10 educators have expressed definitely to me their opposition to it and yet say, "I did not vote that way." I do not see why the fight was not made there if there was strength of opposition. I do not see why some of those men who have said that so definitely to me did not make the fight.

Doctor Machen. It is a very strange thing to me that that is not done. A great many men feel that there is no use in voting against a thing unless you can defeat it. I do not feel that way. I think it is a very important thing to vote exactly in accordance with your conscience, quite irrespective of the immediate success of your vote in your dealing with that measure.

Mr. Holaday. Doctor, do you feel that at any time in the past the present Bureau of Education has directly or indirectly interfered with the operation of the school with which you are connected?

Doctor Machen. No, sir; I do not think that there is anything to be said definitely with respect to the theological school with which I am connected.

Mr. Holaday. Do you know whether or not the Bureau of Education has ever interfered, directly or indirectly, with the operation of any private or church school?

Doctor Machen. I have not the evidence before me. I myself am inclined to think that the classification of colleges which has been proposed by it is unfortunate, and I believe that the vast enlargement of such activities by a department of education would be dangerous; but I am not in the present hearing at all personally interested with respect to my activities in the institution with which I am connected.

With respect to the future, I do feel, sir, that I am contending for a principle which is absolutely necessary to the principle of religious liberty. There are in the sphere of education tendencies which are directly opposed to religious liberty, such as the effort to produce a system of morality codes, etc., in the public schools; and the whole notion that the function of the public school is to be enlarged it seems to me is inimical to the principle of parental authority, and is very dangerous. The proper tendency, it seems to me, would be to diminish rather than to increase the function of the public school, and to place the responsibility for the moral and religious training of children exactly where it belongs, upon the individual parents. There is a tendency there which I think is dangerous; and the tendency of those who advocate this bill, with their desire that there shall be a dignity given to public education under central control which it does not possess, that its function shall be enlarged, if continued, I think, will be inimical in the most thoroughoing way to religious liberty.

Mr. Reed of New York. Doctor, may I ask you a question? Carrying out your principle, if it were left to you, would you abolish the present Bureau of Education entirely?

Doctor Machen. I could not say that definitely until I examine in detail, sir, all of the functions of the present Bureau of Education. It is perfectly obvious that the Federal Government has some functions in the sphere of education, for instance in the District of Columbia; and I should have to inform myself more particularly before I could answer that question. But I do advocate the abolition of certain functions of the present Bureau of Education, its activities as a general agency in the guidance of the States in their own individual affairs. I think that there are activities which would far better be avoided; but I cannot make so sweeping an assertion as that I should advocate the abolition of the Bureau of Education without examining all of its functions.

Mr. Reed of New York. I know that you are sincere in opposing it on principle, not only in education, but in other activities. For instance, we will take the Department of Agriculture. Carrying out your principle, if you had the right to do it, would you be in favor of eliminating Federal aid in the Agricultural Department?

Doctor Machen. I think this is to be said—that when you eliminate an agency which has long been in operation you are doing something more serious than the avoidance of an entrance upon those activities; and I should have to examine the dangers which might result from the sudden elimination of such activities in the sphere of agriculture. I do feel, however, that there is a difference between the sphere of education and those other spheres. As I say, I think that when it comes to the training of human beings, you have to be a great deal more careful than you do in other spheres about preservation of the right of individual liberty and the principle of individual responsibility; and I think we ought to be plain about this—that unless we preserve the principles of liberty in this department there is no use in trying to preserve them anywhere else. If you give the bureaucrats the children, you might as well give them everything else as well. [Applause.]

So that it does seem to me we are dealing with the most important part of human life when we are dealing with education, and we are dealing with a sphere where analogies drawn from mechanical spheres are very dangerous; and yet I am opposed in general to the notion that even in other spheres we should develop the principle that if someone else does not do it, Washington will always step in and do it. I think that is opposed to an economical conduct of life; it is working great moral harm to our people in many other spheres; but the exact limits of the activities of the Federal Government constitute a question with which I am not now attempting to deal.

I have tried to observe, in the sphere of education, the results of the present tendency toward standardization, and I think those results are lamentable. I think we are having to-day a very marked intellectual as well as moral decline through the gradual extension of this principle of standardization in education. People are ready to admit to some extent that there is a sort of moral decline, but what is not always observed is that there is a terrible intellectual decline, and that intellectual decline comes through the development of this principle of unification and standardization to which I object; for I think that in the sphere of education uniformity always means not something uniformly high but something uniformly low.

Mr. Holaday. Doctor, I understood you to say that in your opinion the public schools have already gone too far in moral teaching. I should like a little further information about your ideas on that question.

Doctor Machen. I am not sufficiently familiar with the actual working out of these proposals in detail; but I am opposed in general to the morality codes which have been proposed here in Washington, for example, which represent morality as the result of human experience, and so seem to me to undermine the very basis of morality and to be producing moral decline. My position with regard to moral and religious training in its connection with the State is rather simple. I think it is a very good thing if the public schools release children at convenient hours during the week for religious training, but I am absolutely opposed to any granting of school credit for work done in those hours, to the slightest scrutiny of attendance or of the standards of instruction, or anything of the kind; and I hold that the solution of our difficulties is in the restriction in general of the public schools to their function of imparting knowledge, and the gradual production in the minds of our people of the notion that moral and religious training is a responsibility of the parents and not of the State.

I do not know, sir, whether that answers your question.

Mr. Holaday. I think so.

Mr. Robison. Mr. Chairman, I should like to ask the witness a few questions.

What is the nature of your work at Princeton?

Doctor Machen. I am a professor in Princeton Theological Seminary, which is an institution for the training of ministers.

Mr. Robinson. I understand that, but what is your particular work in that institution?

Doctor Machen. I am a teacher in the New Testment department.

Mr. Robison. Have you ever had any experience in teaching in the public schools?

Doctor Machen. No, sir. I have had an experience of the result of such activities—a rather wide experience.

Mr. Robison. Have you ever had any experience in directing the public-school work of any community or State?

Doctor Machen. No, sir.

Mr. Robison. Your fear is that this department of education would have a tendency to federalize or centralize and enslave the public-school system of the Nation?

Doctor Machen. Yes, sir.

Mr. Robison. And then I take it, as a logical result or sequence, that you are opposed to the present Bureau of Education in so far as it acts as a fact-finding organization, or gives leadership and stimulation, or undertakes to do so, to the public-school work of the Nation?

Doctor Machen. I am not entirely prepared to answer that question categorically.

Mr. Robison. I mean, outside the District of Columbia.

Doctor Machen. There are a good many functions in the sphere of education which legitimately belong to the Federal Government; but I am opposed to the extension of an agency which assists the States and assists private individuals, or a Federal agency even in the spheres about which you are speaking.

Mr. Robison. So that we may understand each other and so that we may understand your testimony, what spheres do you think are properly occupied by the Federal Government, or could be, so far as its relations to the public schools in the States, outside of the District of Columbia, are concerned?

Doctor Machen. I am inclined to think that it would have been better if it had not entered on that field at all.

Mr. Robison. No; you said you were in favor of some things. I want to know what those things are.

Doctor Machen. I mentioned one—the District of Columbia.

Mr. Robison. Outside of the District of Columbia? We make laws here for the District of Columbia, and make the laws of the Federal Government.

Doctor Machen. I hate to speak about a subject where I have not all of the facts in hand, and I am not speaking in general about detailed activities of the Federal Bureau of Education. Until I am asked about every one of those activities separately I should not like to make general statements about them.

Mr. Robison. But your statement was, if I understood you, that you thought there were spheres in which the Federal Government could and should properly participate in public education outside of the District of Columbia. My inquiry is, What are those spheres? What should it do properly?

Doctor Machen. Well, sir, I do not feel that I can undertake the rather difficult duty of mapping a program for a Federal agency. I am speaking only in opposition to something. I am not speaking in favor of other things or mapping out a legitimate program.

Mr. Robison. But I asked that question because of your statement that the Federal Government had proper spheres in public education outside of the District of Columbia. I am merely inquiring what are those spheres in your mind?

Doctor Machen. I do not know that I made that assertion, sir—that the Federal Government has proper spheres for education outside of the District of Columbia. I am not saying that it has not, and I am not saying that it has, sir.

Mr. Robison. Then you have not made sufficient investigation to know whether these activities of the Bureau of Education have been helpful or harmful to the public schools of the Nation? Is not that your position?

Doctor Machen. I think it is quite possible that some of

those activities have been helpful; but I am opposed to the increase of the functions of this Federal agency because that increase is distinctly in the interest of a general aid carried on by the Federal Government in the sphere of the individual States, and I am sorry that such a Federal agency is already in existence. I am sorry that that part of Fereral activities has already begun. I think it is perfectly proper for the Federal Government to maintain here in Washington certain museums and certain agencies for education in the National Capital. I think a good many of those activities may be of benefit to the people of the whole country, and I am not attempting to draw the line in any clear way.

Mr. Robison. Now, if I understand you, if you are sorry that there is a Bureau of Education here in Washington, then it follows that your mind tells you that it ought to be abolished; and then, further, if you do not know the activities of the Bureau of Education here and its relation to the public schools and public education of the country, how can you say that an enlargement of this bureau would be harmful or helpful?

Doctor Machen. I am opposed to it, as I tried to explain, sir, in principle.

Mr. Robison. I know you said you are opposed to it.

Doctor Machen. I am opposed to the principle of Federal aid, and I am opposed to the activities of the Federal bureau where they involve the laying down of standards of education —of certain standards for colleges, for example. I think that is an unfortunate thing. I think it is very much better to have men who are engaged in education examine methods of education, examine standards, rather than to have such agencies of research come before the people with the authority of the Federal Government, with the fear at all times that we shall have an agitation to compel schools to maintain those standards. We have very frequently the principle that the States are to be allowed to do this and that; but if they do not maintain certain standards which have been laid down by Federal agencies of research, they should then be compelled to do it by some sort of an amendment to the Constitution or the like.

Mr. Robison. I want you to point out what section of this bill in your opinion would give the Federal Government control or direction of any public school or, for that matter, any private school in any State or community.

Doctor Machen. This provision at the beginning of it—that there is established at the seat of Government an executive department to be known as the department of education. That I think, establishes an extent of Federal activity in principle which will be deleterious, which will lead to a great many activities in the future. If you have a Federal department of education that has a place in the Cabinet, you have a department which is going to extend constantly its activities and is going to ask for more and more funds. We have, of course, an illustration of this in the extremely radical bill which is now in Congress which would extend this principle of Federal aid to the States and which lays down the conditions upon which that Federal aid is to be received. That has always been in connection with this demand for this establishment of a Federal department of education, and I think it is in organic connection with it. The very establishment of a Federal department of education, I think, is dangerous, because it will lead to such measures as those which have been proposed for a great many years, which provide for Federal aid on a large scale.

Mr. Robison. Do you believe that Congress has the power to pass any law that would give the Federal Government control of the public schools in any State?

Doctor Machen. I think the powers of the Federal Government in this respect under the Constitution may be doubtful; but I think that there are indirect ways of establishing this unification which are very effective and which are very disastrous.

Now, of course there is another specific portion of this bill which provides for the activities to which I object:

> The department of education shall collect such statistics and facts as shall show the condition and progress of education in the several States and in foreign countries—

And so forth. And then there is assistance in devising methods of operation.

In the revised form of this bill, Senate bill 2841, we have, as I say, the purpose of such activity explicitly stated—

Senator Copeland. Where is that?

Doctor Machen. It is section 5 of Senate bill 2841:

> The department of education shall * * * with the consent of the advisory board hereafter mentioned, attempt developing a more uniform and efficient system of public common-school education.

I am opposed to a more uniform system of public common-school education. That is explicit in this revised form of the bill, and I think it is clearly implicit in the section to which I have referred.

Mr. Robison. There is nothing compulsory there, is there?

Doctor Machen. There is nothing compulsory in form, but I think there is an establishment of uniformity which has already gone to disastrous lengths in this country, and the encouragement of which I think is a very unfortunate thing. The proper way in which suggestions as to educational standards should come before the authorities of schools is without the extraneous authority of the Federal Government, which, because of the tendency which has been operative in recent years, is far more than merely advisory; it contains all the time an implied threat, you see, and for that reason is very unfortunate.

Senator Ferris. I should like to ask one question.

Senator Phipps. Certainly, Senator.

Senator Ferris. For my own information I wish to ask what you regard as the basic element or elements in moral conduct. Perhaps that is a foolish question.

Doctor Machen. The basic elements in moral conduct?

Senator Ferris. Yes, sir. What is the basis. I judge from your remarks that experience received minor consideration.

Doctor Machen. Yes, sir—Well, I am an adherent of a certain religious group. We have our definite notion as to the basis of morality, and it is in my belief altogether a religious one. I intend to proclaim that basis of morality is the will of God as revealed by God, and I am interested in the right of all others to maintain that as the only basis of morality. I belong to what is often called a very strict sect, the Presbyterian Church, but it is a sect which has always been devoted to the principles of liberty; and I am unlike a great many of my fellow citizens—tolerance to me means not only tolerance for that with which I am agreed, but it means also tolerance for that to which I am most violently opposed.

I was thoroughly opposed, for example, to the Lusk laws in the State of New York which were intended to bring about the closing of the Rand School in the city of New York. I cannot imagine anything more harmful than the Rand School; there is nothing to which I am more opposed, which I think more subversive of morality; and yet I was absolutely opposed to any such law as that. I believe in liberty, and, therefore, when I believe I have a right to proclaim the basis of morality which I think is only in the will of God, I also claim the right for other persons to proclaim whatever else they may hold with regard to it. But to proclaim in our public schools that morality is only the result of human experimentation—"this is the conduct which Uncle Sam has found in the course of American history to be right"—that, I think, is subversive of morality; and I do not believe that anyone can encourage moral conduct in others unless he has first in his own mind the notion of an absolute distinction and not a merely relative distinction between right and wrong.

I do not know whether that at all answers your question.

Senator Ferris. I am just wondering whether there is any such thing as moral conduct in the United States Congress or among the citizens of the United States apart from a distinctively religious basis. I am just wondering whether the public schools have any function in the way of teaching morality which is not distinctively religious in its basic idea.

Doctor Machen. I think that the solution lies not in a theoretic teaching in the public schools as to the basis of morality, because I do not think you can keep that free from religious questions; but I do hold that a teacher who himself or herself is imbued with the absolute distinction between right and wrong can maintain the moral standing, the moral temper of a public school.

Senator Ferris. Is the ethical culturist ruled out from the consideration of morality in his views and conduct?

Doctor Machen. I am not ruling out anybody at all, sir— the ethical culturist or anyone else.

Senator Ferris. No; but if religion is the basic element in all morality, then can we have a morality that is not founded on a religious idea?

Doctor Machen. I myself do not believe that you can have such a morality permanently, and that is exactly what I am interested in trying to get other people to believe; but I am not at all interested in trying to proclaim that view of mine by any measures that involve compulsion, and I am not interested in making the public school an agency for the proclamation of such a view; but I am interested in diminishing rather than increasing the function of the public school, in order to leave room for the opportunity of a propagation of the view that I hold in free conflict with all other views which may be held, in order that in that way the truth finally may prevail.

Senator Phipps. Thank you, Doctor. [Applause.]

Senator Phipps. The next witness will be Dr. Frank J. Goodnow, president of Johns Hopkins University.

8

The Christian School
The Hope of America*

Men Versus Machines

What is the purpose of education? One view which has been widely held is that the purpose of education is to enable a man or a woman to earn more money after graduation from school or college. That is the so-called vocational view of education. Advocates of it can adduce statistics, I believe, to show that graduates of high schools or colleges get better positions than those who are not graduates. With regard to this vocational view it can be said for one thing that it is enormously over-done. It is training up so many people in the hope of their earning large salaries that there are not enough large salaries to go around. That was true even before the depression came upon us. Moreover, this view is hopelessly narrow and inflexible. It seeks to make men efficient machines; but unfortunately a machine can do only one thing, and when that thing no longer needs to be done the machine has to be scrapped. But the deeper objection to the exclusively vocational view of education is that a man never was meant to be a machine at all. If you make a machine of him, you are doing the direct opposite of what true education ought to do.

---

*From *The Christian School the Out-Flowering of Faith.* Chicago: National Union of Christian Schools, 1934.

124

A better view of education is that education ought to broaden a man, ought to keep him from getting into the narrow rut of any one aptitude or activity. I remember that Dr. R.J.G. McKnight, President of the Reformed Presbyterian Seminary in Pittsburgh, in an address which he delivered recently at Westminster Seminary, said that he had made a visit a short time before to an automobile factory. He had admired very much, he said, the wonderful skill developed by operatives in the factory. Particularly had he observed the speed and accuracy with which a man in the assembling plant put on the rear fenders of the cars as they came down the endless line. That man, he said, might not be able to do a lot of other things; but one thing certainly could be said for him—he was certainly the world's best Ford-car-left-rear-fender-putter-on. Well, I think perhaps there is some hope even for that putter on of left rear fenders. With shorter hours and consequently increased leisure given to operatives in factories, it is quite possible that that Ford-car-left-rear-fender-putter-on may learn to love his Tennyson and his Horace in his leisure time.

But whatever may be said of him, it is a poor view of education to hold that it condemns men to remain mere Ford-car-left-rear-fender-putters-on all their lives. I think the man who above all others should be pitied is the man who has never learned how to amuse himself without mechanical assistance when he is alone. Even babies are sometimes taught to amuse themselves. I remember when I was at Princeton I used to watch the baby of one of the professors on the Seminary campus. That self-reliant little mite of humanity would spend the entire morning in the middle of that great green expanse, all by himself, and yet in the most complete contentment and in the most perfect safety. He was early learning the great lesson how to use his leisure time. He did not need to have anybody else rattle his rattle for him. Thank you, if he needed a rattle at all he could rattle his own rattle for himself. He was getting a good preparation for life. A person who can rattle his own rattle when he is a baby is very apt to be able to paddle his own canoe when he becomes a man.

The average American, however, remains a baby all his life. He is unable even to rattle his own rattle. He has to have somebody else amuse him all the time. Leave him alone for five minutes, and he has to turn on his radio. It seems to make very little difference to him what the radio gives forth. All he wants is that some kind of physical impact shall be made on his ear-drums—and incidentally on everybody else's ear-drums—just to keep him from having one moment to himself. Turn off his radio even for a moment and the appalling emptiness of his life is at once revealed.

What is the explanation of this emptiness of American life? The explanation is that the average American is not educated. An uneducated man shrinks from quiet. An educated men longs for it. Leave an educated man alone, and he has, for one thing, the never-failing resource of reading. He has that resource in his home; he may even carry it around in his pocket. Mr. Loeb has done more for the cause of true education with his pocket editions of the classics than have the founders of many universities. Even more truly educated is the man who does not need even the prop of pocket editions, but can draw at any moment, in meditation, upon the resources of a well-stocked mind.

But what shall be done for the great hosts of Americans who have never learned how to read with enjoyment, and to whom meditation has become a lost art? What shall be done about the increasing problem of leisure time?

Intrusions of Government

Well, I can tell you one thing that ought not to be done about it. Whatever may be done about it, government certainly ought not to do anything about it. People talk about this great national problem of leisure time. Since it is a national problem, they say, Congress ought to take it up; or, rather, Congress ought to perform its up-to-date function of being a rubber stamp by turning the problem over to some government bureau. So we shall have government directing even our holiday activities for us; government will be telling us not only how we shall work, and how much we shall work, and how much we shall get for our work, but also how we shall play.

I remember the first school I attended. It was a private school, which, I suppose, might be called a kindergarten. There were various tasks to be performed in the various periods of the school's session. But to me the most irksome period was one in which we were all required to stand up under the eye of the teacher and play games with a lot of little girls. I thought it was the toughest duty of the entire school day. Some time later, years later I think, I discovered that it was supposed to be the recess hour! What I had held to be work was regarded by the teachers as play. I am inclined to think still that I rather than the teachers was right. Play that is prescribed and supervised by the powers that be is often the most irksome kind of work.

That is true of the grandiose recreation schemes into which the Federal government is now entering. A great system of National Parks has been built up. It might have been a beneficent thing if it meant that the natural beauty of the regions now embraced in the National Parks were to be preserved. But as a matter of fact it means nothing of the kind. During a period of over thirty years I used to go in the summers, with some interruptions, to Mt. Desert Island, Maine. When I first went there it was about the sweetest and most beautiful lake and mountain region that could possibly be imagined. It really seemed as though no human being would have the heart to destroy the delicate charm of those woods. But then came Mr. John D. Rockefeller, Jr. and the Lafayette (later Acadia) National Park, and all was changed. Huge roads now scar practically every mountainside and skirt the shores of practically every lake. The woods near the roads have been ruthlessly "cleaned up." The natural beauty of the region has been systematically destroyed. When I go into that National Park, with its dreary regularity and its officialdom, I almost feel as though I were in some kind of penal institution. I feel somewhat as I do when I am in Los Angeles or any of the other over-regulated cities of the West, where pedestrians meekly wait around on the street corners for non-existent traffic and cross the streets only at the sound of the prison gong. Certain it is at any rate that the best way to destroy true recreation is for government to go into the business of promoting it.

The far more serious thing, however, is that this odious governmental activity in the destruction of the natural beauty of the woods is only a symbol of what is going on today in the sphere of human life. As the government bureaus are out to destroy every sweet and free and delicate thing in the woods and streams, so they are also out to destroy every sweet and free and delicate thing in the lives of the citizens. The ideal plainly is that we shall be under government tutelage from the cradle to the grave. In the cradle a maternity bureau will have us in its clutches; in the period of our school life we shall be in government schools, which will direct our recreation as well as our studies; after we get through school we shall be subjected to adult education under government control and shall be questioned as to our use of our leisure time. From this dreary goose-step there will be no escape.

Least of all will escape be found in the privacy of the home, for the simple reason that there will be no privacy of the home. The so-called Child Labor Amendment will, if it is ratified, take care of that.

The "Child Labor Amendment"

That amendment masquerades sometimes under the guise of humanitarianism. People have the utterly erroneous notion that it deals only with gainful employment of children or that it is directed against sweat-shop conditions or the like. As a matter of fact, the amendment provides that "the Congress shall have power to limit, regulate and prohibit the labor of persons under eighteen years of age." It provides for the control of labor in the home just as much as labor in factories or workshops, and it gives full power to prohibit such labor altogether as well as to regulate it. A proposal to change the wording of the amendment so as to exclude the home from the scope of the power granted, and a proposal to make the powers include only the control of labor in mines, quarries, mills, workshops, factories, and manufacturing establishments, and a proposal to make the age limit sixteen years instead of eighteen years, and other proposals in the direction of some kind of rational limitation of the powers granted, were all rejected.[1] The amendment as now before the states places the whole lives of the 45,000,000 persons in the United States who are under eighteen years of age under the despotic control of whatever bureaus Congress may set up.

It is evident that that measure is more than an amendment to the Constitution of the United States. Practically it destroys the

[1] See Sterling E. Edmunds, *The Child Labor Amendment and What It Means,* p. 8, to be procured from the National Committee for the Protection of Child, Family, School and Church, Room 912, 1218 Olive St., St. Louis, Missouri.

Constitution; for it takes the formative and most important part of human life away from the states and places it under the central government. The states, by this measure, are practically wiped out; the whole American idea in government is destroyed.

But the measure goes far beyond that. It confers upon Congress powers which no state now possesses. As Senator James A. Reed rightly said on June 2, 1924[2], no state now possesses the right to prohibit all labor of a youth of seventeen years of age. Yet that stupendous power, it is proposed, shall now be granted to Congress. How will it be exercised? Mr. Sterling E. Edmunds, in his informing address "The Child Labor Amendment and What It Means," points out that the actual "plan of enforcement as set out by the Children's Bureau itself, is to permit no person under the age of eighteen years to engage in any work, household, agricultural and industrial, physical or mental, until such person first obtains a federal work certificate" and that "whether such a certificate can be obtained depends upon four requirements: (1) conclusive proof of age; (2) physical ability, which means a large army of physicians; (3) sufficient educational training; (4) kind of work the person wishes to engage in."[3] Do not deceive yourselves about this thing, my friends. If this amendment is ratified, you parents will receive questionnaires from the Federal government about the most intimate affairs of your family life, and you will be put into jail if you fail to reply. Federal agents will have a full right to enter your homes and supervise the simplest things that your children do for you; the springs of their loyalty and kindness to you and to their brothers and sisters will be dried up; all the decency and privacy of your homes will be gone. Incidentally, Christian schools and everything like Christian schools will be throttled out of existence.

---

[2] Quoted by Sterling E. Edmunds, *op. cit.,* p. 10.

[3] Sterling E. Edmunds, *op. cit.,* p. 8.

That is very definitely the tendency, and it is probably to a very large extent the intention, of leading advocates of this amendment. The amendment was drafted, according to Mr. Edmunds, chiefly by Florence Kelly or Mrs. Florence Kelly Wischnewetsky (if she may be called by the name of her divorced Russian husband), of whose activities as a socialist propagandist Mr. Edmunds gives an impressive list.[4] It has been advocated enthusiastically by the radical forces in the United States. No wonder! The notion underlying this measure is the Russian idea that children exist for the State and are the property of the State. That is diametrically opposed to the Christian idea, which is also the truly American idea, that the State exists for the repression of evil-doers and the protection of individual liberty.

The enemies of liberty, who are advocates of this amendment, have quite correctly seen that the chief obstacle to the accomplishment of their ends is found in the family. So it is against the family that they are directing their chief attack. The most dangerous weapon in their attack just now is found in this so-called Child Labor Amendment.

The Present State of the Conflict

The Child Labor Amendment was first submitted to the States in 1924. It was being rushed through, by means of the customary deceptive representation, as though it were merely a humanitarian measure intended to prevent harmful employment of children in industry. But patriotic citizens in Massachusetts got wind of what was going on. There was a referendum vote and the amendment was overwhelmingly rejected in that state. Up to 1927 only four states had ratified it, and up to 1931 only six in all.

---

[4] Sterling E. Edmunds, *op. cit.,* pp.1f.

Then came the depression and the consequent hysteria. Conditions were such as to rend the heart. It was a time of widespread distress. To the enemies of liberty it seemed to be an admirable time to fish in troubled waters; it was an admirable time to use the generous compassion of well-meaning but ignorant people in order to foist upon the country as cruel and heartless a measure as could possibly be conceived. The so-called Child Labor Amendment was revived.

Up to January 1, 1934 it has been ratified by fourteen more states, making twenty in all. Of these twenty ratifications, about six took place after I spoke to you on this same subject at this time last year. Apparently the enemies of free institutions, though they had had to bide their time, were going to work their will after all. It seemed as though the lovers of decency and liberty were asleep. But those forces at last became aroused, and since January 1, 1934, thirteen states have either rejected the amendment or failed to ratify it. In 1935 the battle will be on again. Twenty-four state legislatures meet in regular session in that year, all but two of them convening in the month of January. Only sixteen of these are needed to bring the total number ratifying the amendment up to the requisite number of thirty-six. The proponents of the measure are determined to enter into the battle with renewed zeal, and they have unquestionably powerful weapons in their hands.

I wonder, my friends, whether you realize what a momentous battle this is. The hearts of Frenchmen were stirred when Clemenceau said with regard to the Germans at Verdun: "They shall not pass." But during 1935 we Americans will be engaged in a still more serious battle. Even if the German Empire under Kaiser Wilhelm II was all that its enemies said it was—all that and far more—still it did not begin to be as much opposed to American institutions as are the forces really back of this misnamed Child Labor Amendment. The battle against this attack upon the American home is a more important battle even than Verdun or the Marne.

An Unexpected Ally

I am glad to notice that we have some unexpected allies in that battle. At least we have some unexpected allies in the battle against the real tendency of this amendment, no matter what the attitude of the gentlemen whom I am now going to quote is toward the amendment itself. In the *New York Times* of August 7, 1934, some very sound remarks were reported from an address of one of the most eminent scientists of our day, Dr. Robert A. Millikan, President of the California Institute of Technology. In ringing words Dr. Millikan condemned dictatorship and communism and paternalism. "Some of them call it communism," he said, "some socialism, some something else, but I am using the proper term Stateism to include this whole tendency toward the government's ownership and operation of everything, this whole movement that weakens self-reliance, discourages private initiative, diminishes opportunity, stimulates bonus marches, veterans' rackets, even teachers' Federal lobbies (I admit it with shame)." "The end of too much Stateism," Dr. Millikan said further, "is inevitably the breakdown of both the character of a people and the effectiveness of its government."

I agree with the main points of Dr. Millikan's speech with all my soul. That does not mean that I agree with every word that he utters in this address, even in the passage just quoted. I should not be inclined to single out bonus marches or "veterans' rackets" for special attack—not because I approve of bonus marches or "veterans' rackets," if the latter can rightly be called by that term, but because they are at least so much better than are most of the other lobbies and rackets in favor of Stateism today. But when Dr. Millikan condemns "teachers' Federal lobbies," if that means, as I suppose it does, the lobby especially in favor of a Federal department of education and in favor of Federal aid to state schools, then I am with him heart and soul.

The question arises, however, if things are as bad as Dr. Millikan thinks they are in America and as I agree with him that they are, what is to be done about it. Dr. Millikan is not so very clear on that point. He cherishes apparently the hope that natural science may be of some use. But he has to confess that science, with all its achievements, has not been able to check the rise of Stateism and all the degeneration of which Stateism is both a symptom and a cause. He sounds at one point in his address almost a plaintive note. We scientists have been so good to you, he says in effect, and just look what you have done with the great blessings that we gave you. "Now, just after science," he says, if we may here quote his exact words, "has begun to get man out of his habit of cuddling supinely in the lap of the gods, whining about the decrees of the fates and wasting his time and strength in snake dances to bring rain, when he might be building an irrigation ditch, just after science has begun to get man to standing on his own feet and has taught him to rely more than formerly upon his own efforts, she is somewhat disturbed to find a group of political philosophers and sociologists, some of them in high places, too, who come along now and want to push man back not exactly into the lap of the gods or into the hands of the fates but into the soft bosom of the State." Those are golden words, We sympathize with science in her distress, as that distress is so movingly portrayed by one of the most eminent of modern scientists. It is very sad indeed that all the marvelous achievements of scientific genius should result at last in giving us the Brain Trust. It is very sad that all the struggle of humanity toward enlightenment and freedom should succeed only in producing reaction and slavery like that which is involved in the modern paternalistic State.

The Limitations of Natural Science

But what is the cause of this sad decadence? Dr. Millikan gives no answer to this question in the address of which we are now speaking; but he gives *us* a hint as to what the right answer is, when we read his address from our point of view. That hint is given when he says that science has rescued humanity from sitting helplessly "in the lap of the gods." Science has rescued humanity from the gods—let us ponder that assertion for just a moment. I shall not stop to consider the question whether the assertion is correct. I shall not stop to ask whether it was really natural science that rescued mankind from the lap of the gods. I am strongly inclined to think that true religion also may have had something to do with that work of rescue—true religion based upon the facts presented by the queen of sciences, theology. But suppose Professor Millikan is right thus far. Suppose it was really "science" (in the popular sense of the word) that destroyed the gods. In any case, what is clear is that if science really did that, and if that is all that science did, then it is no wonder that scientific progress is resulting in that decadence of humanity of which Dr. Millikan so movingly and so truly speaks. In fact, I think we can go further. I think we can say that science alone, unless something else goes with science, is bound by an inexorable logic to result just exactly in that decadence which so distresses Dr. Millikan's soul. In fact, science has served to improve enormously the technique of tyranny in our day as over against the cruder tyrannies of fire and sword which reigned in the past. It is in accordance with an inexorable logic that Hitler is practising fiendish wickedness in Germany today in the name of science. The great question is, not who or what destroyed the gods in the belief of mankind, but what shall be put in the place of the gods that have been destroyed.

Shall we put in place of them doctrinaire materialism of the old school or the skeptical pragmatism of more recent years or some pantheizing view which when it appears in eminent scientists of our day is sometimes so incautiously hailed by devout people as a return to the Christian position? Shall one of these things be the substitute for that condition of humanity which prevailed when humanity still regarded itself as sitting in the lap of the gods? Or shall we do something entirely different? When we turn from the gods shall we turn to God? Shall we do what those Thessalonian converts did in the year 50 or 51? Shall we turn from idols to serve the living and true God?

It is this latter answer which is given by the Christian schools. It is not the popular answer; it is an answer which goes counter to the whole temper of our age. But so dreadful are the results of the other answers that surely the advocates of this unpopular answer deserve at least a hearing. Dr. Millikan has not painted in any too dark colors the picture of our times. The fact ought to be perfectly clear to every thoughtful observer that humanity is standing over an abyss. When I say humanity, I include America; indeed I am thinking particularly of America. Russia and Germany are already in the abyss. But how shall it be with our country?

American Liberty

When I utter the word "America," I am uttering a word which still has to me a sort of precious and homelike sound. I am hopelessly out of date in this matter, I know; but I cannot help it. I suppose it is terribly foolish of me; I suppose it is disgustingly sentimental; but I am obliged to confess it. I do love my country. Sometimes I almost wish that I did not love it. The love of it gives me such sorrow when I contemplate its present condition. But somehow I cannot get the love of it quite out of my heart, and I cannot quite get the principles upon which it was founded out of my mind. I believe in those principles still. I believe in the notion that there are certain basic rights of the individual man and the individual family which must never be trampled under foot—never for any supposed advantage of the whole, never because of the supposed necessity of any emergency—certain basic rights like the right of personal freedom, the right of property, the right of privacy of the home, the real freedom of speech and of the press. I believe in the specifically American idea in government—not a nation divided for purposes of administrative convenience into a number of units called states, but a number of indestructible states, each with its inalienable rights, each with its distinctive features, with its own virtues to be cultivated by its own citizens, with its own defects not to be remedied at all unless remedied by its own citizens, and, on the other hand, a Federal government not in possession of any general and unexpressed sovereignty but carefully limited to powers expressly granted it by a Constitution which was not of its own making. I believe in a judiciary not cooperating with any economic or social program, as President Roosevelt has intimated that the judiciary is doing now, but a judiciary resolutely refusing to cooperate, a judiciary quite independent of popular clamor, unswerved by any plea of necessity, interpreting the law and the law alone, upholding the high principles of the Constitution through fair weather and foul, guaranteeing to the humblest citizen his inalienable rights against Congress, against the President, against the overwhelming weight of temporary public opinion.

Today this American liberty of ours is very rapidly being destroyed. In the process of its destruction, we are learning something that we ought to have known perfectly well all along

—namely, that freedom is dependent ultimately upon what is in the hearts of the people. Freedom is not safe if it is written only with ink in the Constitution. It must be written also in the fleshy tables of the heart. No country can be permanently free unless the love of freedom is ingrained in the very souls of its people.

Be it observed, moreover, that the love of freedom involves the hatred of something else. It involves the hatred of restraint, the hatred of governmental interference, the hatred of inquisitorial measures of all kinds, the hatred of any undue interference with the privacy of individual citizens or individual families, the profound conviction that government, though necessary, is a necessary evil, not intended to produce blessedness or happiness but intended to prevent blessedness or happiness from being interfered with by wicked men. I think it can be said that no people is fit to govern itself if it does not hate to be governed.

That healthy hatred of being governed, formerly so strong in the American people, is gradually being lost. No interference is resented today, no menace to family life, no government monopoly, if only it be thought to confer physical benefits. I do not think that we ought to deceive ourselves about this matter. We are witnessing today in America the decay of free institutions, and that decay is proceeding quite in the well worn track which it followed, for example, when the Roman Republic gave place to the Roman Empire about two thousand years ago.

Liberty and the Law of God

Upon what were our free institutions founded? I believe that they were founded largely upon a belief in the living God. When I say that I know that objection may be raised by some students of history. Thomas Jefferson, I know, was a freethinker; and yet Thomas Jefferson quite rightly held that the least governed people is the best governed. Yet I am not afraid to say that our free institutions were founded upon belief in God, as God is made known to us through the revelation recorded in the Bible; at least I am not afraid to say that that belief in God was their only sure and lasting foundation. Liberty has sometimes been furthered for the moment by those who do not thus believe in God; but in the long run that is a liberty which turns inevitably to slavery. How shallow was the use of the shibboleth of "Liberty, Equality and Fraternity" at the time of the French Revolution! There is a misinterpretation of equality which makes equality the enemy of real freedom. If you crush out individuality by the strong arm of the State, then ultimately the state will be all, and the individual and the family will be nothing, and liberty will be destroyed.

The fact is, I think, that two strains can be observed in the production of our free institutions. One strain was a mere free-thinking revolt against tyranny like that revolt which was so powerful, for example, later, in the French Revolution; the other was a fear of God which prevented those who had it from being at all afraid of men. Both these strains did immediate service in the production of our civil and religious freedom. But one was permanent and one was not. One led logically to a truly free State and a free school in a free State; the other led logically to collectivism like that which is now being practised in Russia. Human liberty in the long run, even in the mundane sphere of political life, is intimately connected with the deeper liberty of the sons of God.

What do we find in this present-day America, in which the achievements of centuries are so rapidly being lost and in which that liberty which our fathers won at such cost is being thrown away recklessly by one mad generation? I think the really

significant thing that we find is that America has turned away
from God. In the political and social discussions of the day,
God's law has ceased to be regarded as a factor that deserves to
be reckoned with at all. That is true in regard to the higher
ranges of human life; it is also true in regard to that mammon in
which our Lord said a man must be faithful if he is to be faithful
in higher things. We hear much about mammon today: we hear
much about the currency; we hear much about the question
whether what is euphemistically called a "managed currency"
is or is not economically more advantageous than the gold
standard. But the sad thing is that in all this discussion we hear
little about simple honesty, which is the law of God. I can
remember when I had a certain patriotic pride in the good faith
of the United States government, in those bygone days when the
phrase "sound as a dollar" had not yet become a jest. The
United States government, in its business dealings, seemed to
me to be the very embodiment of integrity; I regarded it as
almost inconceivable that it would repudiate its corporate
obligations. Yet today it has done just that. Of course, there are
times when a government or an individual must fail to meet
obligations. That is when the government or the individual is
bankrupt, when the government or the individual acknowl-
edges the justice of the obligations but is under the necessity of
pleading that they cannot be met. I am not saying, therefore,
that when a country goes off the gold standard it is necessarily
acting dishonestly. But it is not such an honest bankruptcy
which we have in the United States at the present time. On the
contrary, what we have is a very ruthless application of the
devil's principle that "might makes right." Look at a United
States gold certificate, if you can find one somewhere in a
museum today without being put in jail for looking at it. Upon it
the United States government promises to pay very specifically
not in some other currency but in gold. It is a solemn obligation

of the United States. It is a solemn contract, not of any individual, but of the United States government, a contract to the fulfilment of which the honor of the American people is pledged, a contract with the holder of the note. Today not only is that contract not fulfilled, but the holder of the contract is threatened with imprisonment unless he hands over to the defaulting party the contract itself.

I tell you, my friends, there are many things that are uncertain about the future; but of one thing we can be sure—a nation that tramples thus upon the law of God, that tramples upon the basic principles of integrity, is headed for destruction unless it repents in time. We hear much about the menace of gangdom and kidnappers today. To meet that menace opponents of American liberty are proposing all sorts of extreme measures. They are proposing, for example, that all citizens shall be fingerprinted and that a system of police surveillance shall be set up in this country. Pray God that these proposals may be rejected and the remnants of American liberty may as long as possible be preserved! But the real reason why young men fall into crime is that the law of God is so generally disobeyed. When the government itself lends itself to a sort of glorified robbery, what can be expected from the impressionable youth of the day? If solemn contracts, public and private, are mere scraps of paper, if sheer power is everything, if that principle is operative in high places, who can wonder if it is put into operation also in individual lives? The real evil is the same in both cases. The real evil is the ruthless disregard of the law of God.

That disregard is becoming more and more blatant. Ten or fifteen years ago the spectacle of two Reno divorces in the best-known family in the land, and the spectacle of the mother in that family telling other people how to bring up their children and advocating an amendment to the Constitution which would govern the most intimate affairs of family life—not so very long ago such spectacles would have affected the American people with a wholesome disgust. At present they seem to be regarded very much as a matter of course.

Amid this welter of lawlessness, public and private, in the face of this slavery which is not the enemy of lawlessness but its twin sister, where shall we find a nursery of decency and freedom and gentleness and honesty and bravery and peace? I have no hesitation in saying that we can find such a nursery in the Christian schools.

The Value of the Christian Schools

The Christian schools ought indeed to be welcomed even from the point of view of a merely secular broadening of the mind. They ought to be welcomed by every friend of real education simply because they tend to liberate our people from the dead hand of monopolistic state control which keeps education in a miserable rut and checks true intellectual advance. Even in their mere capacity as private schools they are worthy of all support.

But incomparably greater is their value as *Christian* schools. As Christian schools they are like a precious salt amid our people, a precious salt that checks the ravages of decay; as Christian schools, too, they offer blessings with which all the blessings of this world are not worthy to be compared; they offer a liberty of which that lost civil liberty, regarding which we have been speaking tonight, is but a by-product; they offer the liberty with which Christ has made us free.

One word more needs to be spoken. What has Christianity to do with education: What is there about Christianity which makes it necessary that there should be Christian schools?

Very little, some people say. Christianity, they say, is a life, a temper of soul, not a doctrine or a system of truth; it can provide its sweet aroma, therefore, for any system which secular education may provide; its function is merely to evaluate whatever may be presented to it by the school of thought dominant at any particular time.

This view of the Christian religion, I need not point out in this company, is radically false. Christianity is, indeed, a way of life; but it is a way of life founded upon a system of truth. That system of truth is of the most comprehensive kind; it clashes with opposing systems at a thousand points. The Christian life cannot be lived on the basis of anti-Christian thought. Hence the necessity of the Christian school.

In a book written by two radically skeptical writers, John Herman Randall and John Herman Randall, Jr., there is an interesting passage. "Evangelical orthodoxy," say these skeptical writers, "thrives on ignorance and is undermined by education; Catholic orthodoxy is based on conviction, and has an imposing educational system of its own."[5] Is that dictum of these brilliant skeptical writers true? I am bound to say that it may seem to have certain sting of truth about it. When we contemplate a type of Protestant orthodoxy that is content to take forlorn little shreds of Christian truth and tag them here and there upon a fundamentally anti-Christian or non-Christian education, and when we contrast such a procedure with the great system of Roman Catholic schools and the serious, comprehensive effort which the Roman Catholic Church makes to inform and mould human life, we can well understand the contrast so humiliating to Protestantism, which the Randalls have so forcibly drawn. Yet the dictum is not true; and in proof of the the fact that it is not true I point tonight, as I

---

[5] John Herman Randall and John Herman Randall, Jr., *Religion and the Modern World*, 1929, p. 136.

would point in any company, to your Christian schools. You at least are seeking to oppose a Christian system to the system of this world; you at least are not making the huge mistake of trying to found the gold and silver and brass and iron of Christian theological seminaries or Christian colleges upon the clay feet of non-Christian schools; you at least are not appealing to ignorance, but you believe that real Christianity should have an educational system of its own. God grant that other Christian people may follow your example! You are the torch-bearers of real advance for the whole Protestant Church. You have pointed out the way. God grant to others the grace to follow you! Thus and thus only will the darkness of ignorance be dispelled and the light of Christian truth be spread abroad in the land.

9

Westminster Theological Seminary:
Its Purpose and Plan*

Westminster Theological Seminary, which opens its doors to-day, will hardly be attended by those who seek the plaudits of the world or the plaudits of a worldly church. It can offer for the present no magnificent buildings, no long-established standing in the ecclesiastical or academic world. Why, then, does it open its doors; why does it appeal to the support of Christian men?

The answer is plain. Our new institution is devoted to an unpopular cause; it is devoted to the service of One who is despised and rejected by the world and increasingly belittled by the visible church, the majestic Lord and Saviour who is presented to us in the Word of God. From him men are turning away one by one. His sayings are too hard, his deeds of power too strange, his atoning death too great an offense to human pride. But to him, despite all, we hold. No Christ of our own imaginings can ever take his place for us, no mystic Christ whom we seek merely in the hidden depths of our own souls. From all such we turn away ever anew to the blessed written Word and say to the Christ there set forth, the Christ with whom then we have living communion: "Lord, to whom shall we go? Thou hast the words of eternal life."

---

* Address delivered at the opening of Westminster Seminary in Witherspoon Hall, Philadelphia, Wednesday, September 25, 1929.

145

The Bible, then, which testifies of Christ, is the centre and core of that with which Westminster Seminary has to do. Very different is the attitude of most theological institutions to-day. Most seminaries, with greater or less clearness and consistency, regard not the Bible alone, or the Bible in any unique sense, but the general phenomenon of religion as being the subject-matter of their course. It is the duty of the theological student, they maintain, to observe various types of religious experience, attested by the Bible considered as a religious classic, but attested also by the religious conditions that prevail to-day, in order to arrive by a process of comparison at that type of religious experience which is best suited to the needs of the modern man. We believe, on the contrary, that God has been pleased to reveal himself to man and to redeem man once for all from the guilt and power of sin. The record of that revelation and that redemption is contained in the Holy Scriptures, and it is with the Holy Scriptures, and not merely with the human phenomenon of religion, that candidates for the ministry should learn to deal.

There is nothing narrow about such a curriculum; many and varied are the types of intellectual activity that it requires. When you say that God has revealed himself to man, you must in the first place believe that God is and that the God who is is one who can reveal himself, no blind world-force, but a living Person. There we have one great division of the theological course. "Philosophical apologetics" or "theism," it is called. But has this God, who might reveal himself, actually done so in the way recorded in the Scriptures of the Old and New Testaments? In other words, is Christianity true? That question, we think, should not be evaded; and what is more, it need not be evaded by any Christian man. To be a Christian is, we think, a truly reasonable thing; Christianity flourishes not in obscurantist darkness, where objections are ignored, but in the full light of day.

But if the Bible contains a record of revelation and redemption, what in detail does the Bible say? In order to answer that question, it is not sufficient to be a philosopher: by being a philosopher you may perhaps determine, or think you can determine, what the Bible ought to say; but if you are to tell what the Bible does say, you must be able to read the Bible for yourself. And you cannot read the Bible for yourself unless you know the languages in which it was written. We may sometimes be tempted to wish that the Holy Spirit had given us the Word of God in a language better suited to our particular race, in a language that we could easily understand; but in his mysterious wisdom he gave it to us in Hebrew and in Greek. Hence if we want to know the Scriptures, to the study of Greek and Hebrew we must go. I am not sure that it will be ill for our souls. It is poor consecration indeed that is discouraged by a little earnest work; and sad is it for the church if it has only ministers whose preparation for their special calling is of the customary superficial kind.

We are not conducting a school for lay workers at Westminster Seminary, useful though such a school would be, but a theological seminary; and we believe that a theological seminary is an institution of higher learning whose standards should not be inferior to the highest academic standards that anywhere prevail.

If then, the students of our seminary can read the Bible not merely in translations, but as it was given by the Holy Spirit to the church, then they are prepared to deal intelligently with the question of what the Bible means. There we have the great subject of Biblical exegesis or Biblical interpretation. I hesitate to use that word "interpretation;" for it is a word that has been the custodian of more nonsense, perhaps, than any other word in the English language to-day. Every generation, it is said, must interpret the Bible and the creeds of the church in its own way. So it is said in effect by many modern leaders of the church: "We accept the Apostles' Creed, but we must interpret the Apostles' Creed in a way that will suit the modern mind. So we repeat the assertion of the Creed, 'The third day he rose again from the dead,' but we interpret that to mean, 'The third day he did not rise again from the dead.' "

In the presence of this modern business of interpreting perfectly plain assertions to mean their exact opposite, do you know what I verily believe? I verily believe that the new Reformation, for which we long, will be like the Reformation of the sixteenth century in that it will mean a return to plain common honesty and common sense. At the end of the middle ages the Bible had become a book with seven seals; it had been covered with the rubbish of the four-fold sense of Scripture and all that. The Reformation brushed that rubbish away. So again to-day the Bible has been covered with an elaborate business of "interpretation" that is worse in some respects than anything that the middle ages could produce. The new Reformation will brush all that away. There will be a re-discovery of the great Reformation doctrine of the perspicuity of Scripture; men will make the astonishing discovery that the Bible is a plain book addressed to plain men, and that it means exactly what it says.

In our work in exegesis at Westminster Seminary, at any rate, we shall seek to cultivate common sense. But common sense is not so common as is sometimes supposed, and for the cultivation of it true learning is not out of place. What a world of vagaries, what a sad waste of time, could be avoided if men would come into contact with the truly fine exegetical tradition of the Christian church! Such contact with the devout and learned minds of the past would not discourage freshness or originality. Far from it; it would help to shake us out of a rut and lead us into fields of fruitful thinking.

In true Biblical exegesis, the Bible must be taken as God has been pleased to give it to the church. And as God has been pleased to give it to the church, it is not a mere text-book of religion written all at one time and in one way. On the contrary, it is composed of sixty-six books written at widely different times and by the instrumentality of widely different men. Let us not regret that fact. If the Bible were a systematic text-book on religion, it would, indeed, possess some advantages: it would presumably be easier to interpret; for much of our present difficulty of interpretation comes from the fact that the Biblical books are rooted in historical conditions long gone by. But if the Bible, under those circumstances, would be easier to interpret, it would speak far less powerfully to the heart of man. As it is, God has been very good. He has given us no cold text-book on religion, but a Book that reaches every heart and answers to every need. He had condescended to touch our hearts and arouse our minds by the wonderful variety and beauty of his Book.

When we have learned to read that Book aright, we can trace the history of the revelation that it sets forth. When we do so, we are engaging in an important part of the theological curriculum. "Biblical theology," it is called. Whether it is set forth in a separate course, or whether it is interwoven, as will probably be done in Westminster Seminary, with the work of the Old and New Testament departments, in either case it is a vital part of that with which we have to deal. "God, who at sundry times and in divers manners spake in time past unto the fathers by the prophets, hath in these last days spoken unto us by his Son"—there is the program of Biblical theology; it traces the history of revelation through Old and New Testament times.

But Biblical theology is not all the theology that will be taught at Westminster Seminary; for systematic theology will be at the very centre of the Seminary's course. At that point an error should be avoided: it must not be thought that systematic theology is one whit less Biblical than Biblical theology is. But it differs from Biblical theology in that, standing on the foundation of Biblical theology, it seeks to set forth, no longer in the order of the time when it was revealed, but in the order of logical relationships, the grand sum of what God has told us in his Word. There are those who think that systematic theology on the basis of the Bible is impossible; there are those who think that the Bible contains a mere record of human seeking after God and that its teachings are a mass of contradictions which can never be resolved. But to the number of those persons we do not belong. We believe for our part that God has spoken to us in his Word, and that he has given us not merely theology, but a system of theology, a great logically consistent body of truth.

That system of theology, that body of truth, which we find in the Bible, is the Reformed Faith, the Faith commonly called Calvinistic, which is set forth so gloriously in the Confession and Catechisms of the Presbyterian Church. It is sometimes referred to as a "man-made creed." But we do not regard it as such. We regard it, in accordance with our ordination pledge as ministers in the Presbyterian Church, as the creed which God has taught us in his Word. If it is contrary to the Bible, it is false. But we hold that it is not contrary to the Bible, but in accordance with the Bible, and true. We rejoice in the approximations to that body of truth which other systems of theology contain; we rejoice in our Christian fellowship with other evangelical churches; we hope that members of other churches, despite our Calvinism, may be willing to enter into Westminster Seminary as students and to listen to what we may have to say. But we cannot consent to impoverish our message by setting forth less than what we find the Scriptures to contain; and we believe that we shall best serve our fellow-Christians, from whatever church they may come, if we set forth not some vague greatest common measure among various creeds, but the great historic Faith that has come through Augustine and Calvin to our own Presbyterian Church. Glorious is the heritage of the Reformed Faith. God grant that it may go forth to new triumphs even in the present time of unbelief!

Systematic theology, on the basis of Holy Scripture, is the very centre of what we have to teach; every other theological department is contributory to that; that department gives a man the message that he has to proclaim. But we have already spoken of the heritage of the Reformed Faith, and of a glorious tradition that has come down to us in the church. And that brings us to speak of another department of the theological curriculum, the department that deals with the history of the Christian church. Our message is based, indeed, directly upon the Bible; we derive the content of it not from the experience of past ages, but from what God has told us in his Word. But it would be a mistake to ignore what past generations, on the basis of God's Word, have thought and said and done. Into many other fields of theological study the study of church history casts a beneficent light. Church history should make us less enthusiastic about a modernity which is really as old as the hills; and amid the difficulties of the present time it should give us new hope. God has brought his church through many perils, and the darkest hour has often preceded the dawn. So it may be in our day. The gospel may yet break forth, sooner than we expect, to bring light and liberty to mankind. But that will be done, unless the lesson of church history is altogether wrong, by the instrumentality, not of theological pacifists who avoid controversy, but of earnest contenders for the faith. God give us men in our time who will stand with Luther and say: "Here I stand, I cannot do otherwise, God help me. Amen."

Thus the minister who goes forth from Westminster

Seminary will, we hope, be a man with a message. He will also, we hope, be a man who can so deliver his message as to reach the hearts and minds of men; and to help him do that, the department of homiletics and practical theology has an important place. It cannot, indeed, itself teach a man how to preach; that he must learn, if at all, by the long experience of subsequent years. But at least it can help him to avoid errors and can start him in the right way; it can start him out in that long course in homiletics which is provided by all the rest of life.

Such, very feebly and imperfectly presented, is the program of Westminster Theological Seminary; it is far better set forth in the fine article which Dr. Oswald T. Allis has recently contributed to *The Sunday School Times.* Many things are omitted from this brief summary of ours. Some of them are omitted because of the imperfections of the speaker or from lack of time. But others are omitted of deliberate purpose. There are many things—many useful things, too—with which a theological seminary should not attempt to deal. Let it never be forgotten that a theological seminary is a school for specialists. We are living in an age of specialization. There are specialists on eyes and specialists on noses, and throats, and stomachs, and feet, and skin; there are specialists on teeth—one set of specialists on putting teeth in, and another set of specialists on pulling teeth out—there are specialists on Shakespeare and specialists on electric wires; there are specialists on Plato and specialists on pipes. Amid all these specialties, we at Westminster Seminary have a specialty which we think in comparison with these others, is not so very small. Our speciality is found in the Word of God. Specialists in the Bible—that is what Westminster Seminary will endeavor to produce. Please do not forget it; please do not call on us for a product that we are not endeavoring to provide. If you want specialists in social science or in hygiene or even in "religion" (in the vague modern sense), then you must go elsewhere for what you want. But if you want men who know the Bible and know it in something more than a layman's sort of way, then call on us. If we can give you such men, we have succeeded; if we cannot give them to you, we have failed. It is a large contract indeed, a contract far too great for human strength. But at least, by God's grace, we shall do our best.

Such is the task of Westminster Theological Seminary. It is a task that needs especially to be undertaken at the present time. Fifty years ago many colleges and universities and theological seminaries were devoted to the truth of God's Word. But one by one they have drifted away, often with all sorts of professions of orthodoxy on the part of those who were responsible for the change. Until May, 1929, one great theological seminary, the Seminary at Princeton, resisted bravely the current of the age. but now that seminary has been made to conform to the general drift. Signers of the Auburn Affirmation, a formal document which declares that acceptance of the virgin birth and of four other basic articles of the Christian faith is non-essential even for ministers, actually sit upon the new governing Board. And they do so apparently with the acquiescence of the rest. Not one word of protest against the outrage involved in their presence has been uttered, so far as I know, by the other members of the Board; and a formal pronouncement, signed by the President of the Seminary and the President of the Board, actually commends the thirty-three members of the Board as men who have the confidence of the church. Surely it is quite clear, in view of that pronouncement, as well as in view of the personnel of the Board, that under such a governing body, Princeton Seminary is lost to the evangelical cause.

At first sight it might seem to be a great calamity; and sad are the hearts of those Christian men and women throughout the world who love the gospel that the old Princeton proclaimed. We cannot fully understand the ways of God in permitting so great a wrong. Yet good may come even out of a thing so evil as that. Perhaps the evangelical people in the Presbyterian Church were too contented, too confident in material resources; perhaps God has taken away worldly props in order that we may rely more fully upon him; perhaps the pathway of sacrifice may prove to be the pathway of power.

That pathway of sacrifice is the pathway which students and supporters of Westminster Seminary are called upon to tread. For that we can thank God. Because of the sacrifices involved, no doubt many have been deterred from coming to us; they have feared the opposition of the machinery of the church; some of them may have feared, perhaps, to bear fully the reproach of Christ. We do not judge them. But whatever may be said about the students who have not come to us, one thing can certainly be said about those who have come—they are real men.

No, my friends, though Princeton Seminary is dead, the noble tradition of Princeton Seminary is alive. Westminster Seminary will endeavor by God's grace to continue that tradition unimpaired; it will endeavor, not on a foundation of equivocation and compromise, but on an honest foundation of devotion to God's Word, to maintain the same principles that the old Princeton maintained. We believe, first, that the Christian religion, as it is set forth in the Confession of Faith of the Presbyterian Church, is true; we believe, second, that the Christian religion welcomes and is capable of scholarly defense; and we believe, third, that the Christian religion should be proclaimed without fear or favor, and in clear opposition to whatever opposes it, whether within or without the church, as the only way of salvation for lost mankind. On that platform, brethren, we stand. Pray that we may be enabled by God's Spirit to stand firm. Pray that the students who go forth from

Westminster Seminary may know Christ as their own Saviour and may proclaim to others the gospel of his love.

Scripture Index

ACTS
2:14-41	*18*
2:42	*35*
16:30-32	*18*

I CORINTHIANS
9:16	*28*
12:21	*26*
13	*30*

GALATIANS
1:8	*28*

GENESIS | *16* |
1:1	*38, 39, 42*
3:17	*41*

ISAIAH
40:11	*42-43*
40:22	*42-43*

JOHN
4:18	*18-19*
6:68	*145*
19:30	*43*

II KINGS
19:14-19	*28*

LUKE
2:49	*43*

MATTHEW
7:11	*23-24*
10:28	*12*
16:23	*27*
18:19	*12*
28:6	*43*

PSALM
19:1	*39*

REVELATION | *16* |

ROMANS
1:20	*39*

I THESSALONIANS
1:9-10	*19*

INDEX

Agriculture, Department of, 113; federal aid to, 109-110
Allis, Oswald T., 152
America, 136
Anti-intellectualism, vii-viii, ix, 2, 13
Apologetics, 22-23, 51-52, 146; and evangelism, 25-26
Apostles' Creed, 148
Arcadia (Lafayette) National Park, 128
Argument, in the Bible, 23-24
Art, 49, 89; and science, 53
Association, right of, 84-85
Athanasius, vii
Atonement, 2, 19
Auburn Affirmation, 153
Augustine, vii, 151

Behaviorism, 88-89, 102
Bible, 7, 8, 25, 26, 29, 38, 40, 42, 53, 139, 146; and argument, 23-24; and contradictions, 150; inerrancy of, ix; interpretation of, 10; perspicuity of, 148; reading in public schools, 64, 78-79
Bible League, 13n., 22
Biblical theology, 149
Black, Loring Milton Jr. (U.S. Representative), 99
Bonus March, 133
Brain Trust, 134

Brookhart, Smith Wildman (U.S. Senator), 99
Brotherhood of man, 60-61
Buck, Pearl S., xi
Bureau of Education, 112, 113, 116, 117, 118
Business, federal aid to, 109

Caesarea-Philippi, 27
California Institute of Technology, 133
Calvin, John, vii, 151
Calvinism, 150
Character education, 61, 76-77; see also Morality codes
Child Labor Amendment, 86, 87, 100, 129-133, 141-142
Child-centered education, 14-15
Children's Bureau, 130
Christian Philosophy of Education, A, (Gordon H. Clark), x, xi
Christian scholarship, importance of, 13-44
Christian schools, 75, 124-144
Christian School, the Out-Flowering of Faith, The, 124n.
Christianity, and reason, 48; and intellect, 54-55; definition of, 142-143; opposed by religious education, 15-16
Christianity and Liberalism (J. Gresham Machen), ix

157

Church, history, 151; schools, 63; unity of, 27, 28
Clark, Gordon H., *Works: A Christian Philosophy of Education,* x, xi
Clemenceau, Georges, 132
Communism, 133
Competition, in education, 64, 94-95, 106-107
Compulsion, 122-123
Conservatives, 5
Contracts, 140-141
Contradictions, in Bible, 150
Controversy, 23-24, 30; and revival, 28
Conversion, 17-19
Copeland, Royal Samuel (U.S. Senator), 99, 120
Creation, 38
Culture, 45-59

Debt, repudiation of, 140-141
Decadence, and science, 135; of America, 66-67
Definition, 1-2
Deity of Jesus Christ, viii
Divinity of Jesus Christ, *see* Deity of Jesus Christ
Doctrinal preaching, 8, 35-36
Doctrine, system of, 42
Downs, Francis Shunk, 9n.

Eaton, 110
Edmunds, Sterling E., *Works: The Child Labor Amendment and What It Means,* 129n., 130, 131
Education, child-centered, 14-15; competition in, 75; department of, 71-73, 84-123; efficiency in, 95-98, 107-108; not a government function, 101-102; practical, 56; purpose of, 90-91, 103, 124-125; study of, 14; uniformity

in, 73-75, 88-91, 100
Edwards, Jonathan, vii
Efficiency, in education, 95-98, 107-108; of federal government, 108
Ellwood, *Works: The Reconstruction of Religion,* 11
Emotionalism, viii
Equal opportunity, 74-75, 95, 106
Evangelism, 13, 16-17, 28, 51; and apologetics, 25-26
Exegesis, grammatico-historical method, 10; of Scripture, 147-149; *see also* Bible
Existentialism, vii
Experience, 1, 21, 22; and morality, 62-63; religious, 1, 146

Faith, viii, 17; and knowledge, 1-12
Family, 131; as educational institution, 8; *see also* Home
Federal aid, to agriculture, 109; to business, 109; to education, 74, 85, 89, 100-101, 106, 109-110, 118-119; to high-ways, 109; to labor, 109
Federal Bureau of Education, 112, 113, 116, 117, 118
Federal department of education, 64, 84-123
Federal government, efficiency of, 108
Federalism, 105, 110-111, 129-130, 137
Ferris, Woodbridge Nathan (U.S. Senator), 99, 121, 122
Fletcher, Thomas Brooks (U.S. Representative), 99
Forward in Faith, 66n.
Franklin, Fabian, 97
Freedom, and prosperity, 67; of education, 94-95

French Revolution, 139
Fundamentalism, 31

German Empire, 132
Germany, 62, 101, 135
God, 2; his existence, 39
Gold standard, 140-141
Goodness, and power, 38
Goodnow, Frank J., 123
Goodspeed, Edgar J., 10
Gospel, 20
Government, necessary evil, 138; purpose of, 131
Government schools, 60-65
Grammatico-historical method, 10; *see also* Exegesis *and* Bible
Great Britain, 110-111
Great depression, 67

Head, and heart, viii
Heresy-hunting, 27
Hezekiah, 28
Highways, federal aid to, 109
History, 3, 47; of church, 151
Hitler, Adolf, 135
Hodge, Caspar Wistar, xi
Hodge, Charles, vii
Holaday, William Perry (U.S. Representative), 99, 112, 114-115
Holy Spirit, 5, 24, 29, 44, 81, 147
Home, as educational institution, 8-9; *see also* Family
Homiletics, 152
Honesty, 140
Hoover, Herbert (President), 72
Horace, 125
House Committee on Education, 72, 99
House of Lords, 104
Housing for the poor, 58

Independence of mind, 4, 5, 6

Inerrancy, of Bible, ix
Infallibility, *see* Inerrancy *and* Bible
Intellect, 2; and Christianity, 54-55; primacy of, 12
Irrationalism, xin.

Jefferson, Thomas, 139
Jesus Christ, 1, 4, 5, 11, 12, 17, 18, 19, 21, 23, 24, 26, 27, 32, 36, 37, 39, 40, 42, 43, 46, 47, 50, 77, 78, 79, 81, 145; divinity (deity) of, viii; resurrection of, 19, 25, 148; virgin birth of, 153
Judiciary, role of, 137
Justification by faith, 10

Kant, Immanuel, vii, ix, 2, 9
Kelly, Florence (Mrs. Florence Kelly Wischnewetsky), 131
Kierkegaard, Soren, vii, ix
Kingdom of God, 50
Knowledge, viii; and faith, 1-12; and piety, 45

Labor, federal aid, to, 109
Lafayette (Arcadia) National Park, 128
Languages, study of, 147
Law, and liberty, 138-140; and sin, 41; of God, 41-42, 65, 138-142· *see also* Moral law
Lawlessness, 141-142; and slavery, 142
Leisure time, problem of, 126-128
Liberalism, religious, vii
Liberty, 138-140; and law of God, 138-140; religious, 112-113
"Liberty, equality, fraternity," 139
Licensing of teachers, 92, 105
Lippmann, Walter, 41
Literature, 3
Loeb, 126

Lord's Prayer, 79
Love, viii
Lowrey, Bill Green (U.S. Representative), 72, 99, 111
Lusk laws, 92, 105, 121
Luther, Martin, vii, 20, 151

Machen, John Gresham, ix, x, xi, xii, 99, 109, 110-123; *Works: Christianity and Liberalism*, ix; *What Is Faith?* ix
Man, 40; brotherhood of, 60-61
Marne, battle of, 133
Marx, Karl, vii
Materialism, 136
McKnight, R.J.G., 125
McReynolds, James Clark (U.S. Supreme Court Justice), 92, 105
Means, Rice William (U.S. Senator), 100
Memorization, 6; *see also* Methodology
Mencken, H.L., xi
Methodology, in education, 3, 6, 72-73, 90; and ignorance, 4; versus content, 14-15
Millikan, Robert A., 133, 134, 135, 136
Miracles, 58
Modernism, 5, 23
Money, 140-141
Moody, Dwight L., 25
Morality, and experience, 76-77, 93; basis of, 121-122
Morality codes, 93, 112, 115; *see also* Character education
Moral law, viii, 93; majesty of, 60; *see also* Law of God
Moses, 21

Napoleonic Wars, 104
National Committee for the Protection of Child, Family, School,

and Church, 129n.
National Education Association, 72, 111
National parks, 127-128
National Union of Christian Schools, 66n., 124
Natural theology, 39, 47
Nebraska, and public education, 68; language law, 92, 104, 105
Neo-orthodoxy, vii
New Testament, and polemics, 29
New York State, and public education, 68, 92, 105
New York Times, The, 133
Nietzsche, Friedrich, vii

Oregon, and public education, 68-69; school law, 92, 104, 105
Originality, 4, 6; *see also* Independence of mind
Orthodox Presbyterian Church, xin.
Owen, John, vii

Pantheism, 136
Parental rights, 91, 98, 101-102, 104, 112; *see also* Family *and* Home
Pasteur, Louis, 93
Patriotism, 136-137; and education, 61-62
Paul, 11, 18, 19, 20, 23, 27, 28, 35; epistles of, 35
Pedagogy, 3, 7, 14; and ignorance, 4; *see also* Methodology
Pentecost, 18, 29, 44
Perspicuity, of Bible, 148
Peter, 18, 27
Philippi, 18, 27
Philosophy, 47; and education, 102
Phipps, Laurence C. (U.S. Senator), 99, 110-111, 121, 123

Piety, and knowledge, 45
Pilate, ix, 2
Pilgrim's Progress, 34-35
Plato, 152; *Works: Republic,* 87, 101
Poetry, 89
Polemics, and New Testament, 29
Positivism, vii
Power, and goodness, 38
Practical men, 45-46
Practical teaching, 7-8
Pragmatism, vii, 136
Prayer, 28
Preaching, of doctrine, 35-36
Predestination, 83
Presbyterian Church, 27, 29, 121, 150, 151, 154
Press, freedom of, 137
Primacy, of intellect, 12
Princeton Theological Review, 9n., 45n.
Princeton Theological Seminary, xi, 37, 45n., 84, 99, 110, 115, 125, 153, 154
Princeton University, 84
Privacy, right of, 137
Private schools, 63, 75; *see also* Christian schools *and* Church schools
Progress, 108-109
Property, right of, 137
Propositional truth, viii; *see also*
Prosperity, and freedom, 67
Protestantism, 143
Prussia, 62
Public education, 60-65, 92-94; and morality codes, 93, 112, 115; as threat to political freedom, 68
Public Schools in England, 110

Radicals, 5

Rand School, 121
Randall, John Herman, *Works: Religion and the Modern World,* 143
Randall, John Herman Jr., *Works: Religion and the Modern World,* 143
Reason, ix, 2; and Christianity, 48
Redemption, 2
Reed, Daniel Alden (U.S. Representative), 99, 113
Reed, James Alexander (U.S. Senator), 130
Reformation, 5, 10, 148
Reformation, new, 6, 15, 29
Reformed Presbyterian Seminary, 125
Regeneration, 24
Regulation of Christian schools, 64
Released-time program, 64, 80
Religion, 16; as experience, 1, 54
Religion and the Modern World (J.H. Randall and J.H. Randall, Jr.), 143
Religious education, 46-47, 80-81; hostile to Christianity, 15-16
Religious liberty, 112-113
Renaissance, new, 6, 15
Republic (Plato), 101
Resurrection of Christ, 19, 25, 148
Revelation, 146
Revival, 5, 28
Rights, of individual, 137
Rimmon, 28
Ritschl, Albrecht, 9
Robison, John Marshall (U.S. Representative), 99, 109, 110, 115
Rockefeller, John D. Jr., 128
Roget's *Thesaurus,* 31
Roman Catholicism, 143

Roman Empire, 88, 101, 138
Roman Republic, 138
Romantic movement, vii
Roosevelt, Franklin Delano
  (President), 137
Rugby, 110
Russia, 101, 136

Salvation, 42
Satan, 27
Saturday Evening Post, The, 32
Scepticism, 15, 16, 80
Schleiermacher, Friedrich, vii, ix,
  2, 9
Scholarship, Christian, 13-44
Science, 3, 46, 47, 75; and deca-
  dence, 135; and technology, 48-
  49; and tyranny, 67-68; limita-
  tions of, 135-136
Self-interest, 41
Seminary education, 51-52, 58,
  145-155; purpose of, 38
Senate Committee on Education
  and Labor, 72, 99
Sentinels of the Republic, 71, 84,
  93, 94
Sermon, purpose of, 59
Shakespeare, William, 152
Silas, 18
Sin, viii, 19, 40, 44, 58; and law,
  41; *see also* Law of God
Sincerity, 96
Slavery, twin of lawlessness, 142
Social action, 58
Socialism, 97, 133
Specialization, 152
Speech, freedom of, 137
Spurgeon, Charles Haddon, 25
Statism, 134
Sterling-Reed Bill, 86, 87
Sunday School Times, The, 152
Syncretism, 80
Systematic theology, 149-151

Teaching, practical and doctrinal,
  7-8
Tennyson, Alfred Lord, 125
Terms, redefinition of, viii-ix
Theology, Biblical, 149; systema-
  tic, 149-151
Thessalonians, 136
Tolerance, 85, 121
Traffic regulations, 128
Trust, 20
Truth, 2, 16; propositional, viii
Tyranny, scientific, 67-68

Uniformity, in education, 86, 100,
  102-103
Union Station, 108
Unity, in church, 27, 28
University, proposed by George
  Washington, 107
U.S. Congress, 71, 85, 99, 122,
  127, 129, 130, 137
U.S. Constitution, 67, 100, 110,
  119, 129, 137, 138, 141
U.S. Supreme Court, 92, 105

Values education, 60-65; *see also*
  Morality codes *and* Character
  education
Van Til, Cornelius, xin.
Verdun, battle of, 132
Veterans, 133
Virgin Birth, of Christ, 153
Voting, 111-112

Washington, George, 107
Wells, H.G., *Works: Outline of
  History*, 88, 101
Westminster Confession of Faith,
  150, 154
Westminster Shorter Catechism,
  40, 150
Westminster Standards, 40-41,
  150, 154

Westminster Theological Semi-
nary, 33, 37-38, 125, 145-155
What Is Faith? (J. Gresham
Machen), ix
Wilhelm, Kaiser II, 132

The Woman Patriot, 84
World War I, 71

Yale Review, 97

The Crisis of Our Time

Historians have christened the thirteenth century the Age of Faith and termed the eighteenth century the Age of Reason. The twentieth century has been called many things: the Atomic Age, the Age of Inflation, the Age of the Tyrant, the Age of Aquarius. But it deserves one name more than the others: the Age of Irrationalism. Contemporary secular intellectuals are anti-intellectual. Contemporary philosophers are anti-philosophy. Contemporary theologians are anti-theology.

In past centuries secular philosophers have generally believed that knowledge is possible to man. Consequently they expended a great deal of thought and effort trying to justify knowledge. In the twentieth century, however, the optimism of the secular philosophers has all but disappeared. They despair of knowledge.

Like their secular counterparts, the great theologians and doctors of the church taught that knowledge is possible to man. Yet the theologians of the twentieth century have repudiated that belief. They also despair of knowledge. This radical skepticism has filtered down from the philosophers and theologians and penetrated our entire culture, from television to music to literature. *The Christian in the twentieth century is confronted with an overwhelming cultural consensus—sometimes stated explicitly, but most often implicitly: Man does not and cannot*

164

know anything truly.

What does this have to do with Christianity? Simply this: If man can know nothing truly, man can truly know nothing. We cannot know that the Bible is the Word of God, that Christ died for sin, or that Christ is alive today at the right hand of the Father. Unless knowledge is possible, Christianity is nonsensical, for it claims to be knowledge. What is at stake in the twentieth century is not simply a single doctrine, such as the Virgin Birth, or the existence of hell, as important as those doctrines may be, but the whole of Christianity itself. If knowledge is not possible to man, it is worse than silly to argue points of doctrine—it is insane.

The irrationalism of the present age is so thorough-going and pervasive that even the Remnant—the segment of the professing church that remains faithful—has accepted much of it, frequently without even being aware of what it was accepting. In some circles this irrationalism has become synonymous with piety and humility, and those who oppose it are denounced as rationalists—as though to be logical were a sin. Our contemporary anti-theologians make a contradiction and call it a Mystery. The faithful ask for truth and are given Paradox. If any balk at swallowing the absurdities of the anti-theologians, they are frequently marked as heretics or schismatics who seek to act independently of God.

There is no greater threat facing the true Church of Christ at this moment than the irrationalism that now controls our entire culture. Communism, guilty of tens of millions of murders, including those of millions of Christians, is to be feared, but not nearly so much as the idea that we do not and cannot know the truth. Hedonism, the popular philosophy of America, is not to be feared so much as the belief that logic —that "mere human logic," to use the religious irrationalists' own phrase—is futile. The attacks on truth, on revelation, on the intellect, and on logic are renewed daily. But note well: The misologists—the haters of logic—use logic to demonstrate the futility of using logic. The anti-intellectuals construct intricate intellectual arguments to prove the insufficiency of the intellect. The anti-theologians use the revealed Word of God to show that there can be no revealed Word of God—or that if there could, it would remain impenetrable darkness and Mystery to our finite minds.

Nonsense Has Come

Is it any wonder that the world is grasping at straws—the straws of experientialism, mysticism and drugs? After all, if people are told that the Bible contains insoluble mysteries, then is not a flight into mysticism to be expected? On what grounds can it be condemned? Certainly not on logical grounds or Biblical grounds, if logic is futile and the Bible unintelligible. Moreover, if it cannot be condemned on logical or Biblical grounds, it cannot be condemned at all. If people are going to have a religion of the mysterious, they will not adopt Christianity: They will have a genuine mystery religion. "Those who call for Nonsense," C.S. Lewis once wrote, "will find that it comes." And that is precisely what has happened. The popularity of Eastern mysticism, of drugs, and of religious experience is the logical consequence of the irrationalism of the twentieth century. There can and will be no Christian revival—and no reconstruction of society—unless and until the irrationalism of the age is totally repudiated by Christians.

The Church Defenseless

Yet how shall they do it? The spokesmen for Christianity have been fatally infected with irrationalism. The seminaries, which annually train thousands of men to teach millions of Christians, are the finishing schools of irrationalism, completing the job begun by the government schools and colleges. Some of the pulpits of the most conservative churches (we are not speaking of the apostate churches) are occupied by graduates of the anti-theological schools. These products of modern anti-theological education, when asked to give a reason for the hope that is in them, can generally respond with only the intellectual analogue of a shrug—a mumble about Mystery. They have not grasped—and therefore cannot teach those for whom they are responsible—the first truth: "And ye shall know the truth." Many, in fact, explicitly deny it, saying that, at best, we possess only "pointers" to the truth, or something "similar" to the truth, a mere analogy. Is the impotence of the Christian Church a puzzle? Is the fascination with pentecostalism and faith healing among members of conservative churches an enigma? Not when one understands the sort of studied nonsense that is purveyed in the name of God in the seminaries.

The Trinity Foundation

The creators of The Trinity Foundation firmly believe that theology is too important to be left to the licensed theologians —the graduates of the schools of theology. They have created The Trinity Foundation for the express purpose of teaching the faithful all that the Scriptures contain—not warmed over, baptized, secular philosophies. Each member of the board of directors of The Trinity Foundation has signed this oath: "I believe that the Bible alone and the Bible in its entirety is the Word of God and, therefore, inerrant in the autographs. I believe that the system of truth presented in the Bible is best summarized in the Westminster Confession of Faith. So help me God."

The ministry of The Trinity Foundation is the presentation of the system of truth taught in Scripture as clearly and as completely as possible. We do not regard obscurity as a virtue, nor confusion as a sign of spirituality. Confusion, like all error, is sin, and teaching that confusion is all that Christians can hope for is doubly sin.

The presentation of the truth of Scripture necessarily involves the rejection of error. The Foundation has exposed and will continue to expose the irrationalism of the twentieth century, whether its current spokesman be an existentialist philosopher or a professed Reformed theologian. We oppose anti-intellectualism, whether it be espoused by a neo-orthodox theologian or a fundamentalist evangelist. We reject misology, whether it be on the lips of a neo-evangelical or those of a Roman Catholic charismatic. To each error we bring the brilliant light of Scripture, proving all things, and holding fast to that which is true.

The Primacy of Theory

The ministry of The Trinity Foundation is not a "practical" ministry. If you are a pastor, we will not enlighten you on how to organize an ecumenical prayer meeting in your community or how to double church attendance in a year. If you are a homemaker, you will have to read elsewhere to find out how to become a total woman. If you are a businessman, we will not tell you how to develop a social conscience. The professing church is drowning in such "practical" advice.

The Trinity Foundation is unapologetically theoretical in its outlook, believing that theory without practice is dead, and that practice without theory is blind. The trouble with the professing church is not primarily in its practice, but in its theory. Christians do not know, and many do not even care to know, the doctrines of Scripture. Doctrine is intellectual, and Christians are generally anti-intellectual. Doctrine is ivory tower philosophy, and they scorn ivory towers. The ivory tower, however, is the control tower of a civilization. It is a fundamental, theoretical mistake of the practical men to think that they can be merely practical, for practice is always the practice of some theory. The relationship between theory and practice is the relationship between cause and effect. If a person believes correct theory, his practice will tend to be correct. The practice of contemporary Christians is immoral because it is the practice of false theories. It is a major theoretical mistake of the practical men to think that they can ignore the ivory towers of the philosophers and theologians as irrelevant to their lives. Every action that the "practical" men take is governed by the thinking that has occurred in some ivory tower—whether that tower be the British Museum, the Academy, a home in Basel, Switzerland, or a tent in Israel.

In Understanding Be Men

It is the first duty of the Christian to understand correct theory—correct doctrine—and thereby implement correct practice. This order—first theory, then practice—is both logical and Biblical. It is, for example, exhibited in Paul's epistle to the Romans, in which he spends the first eleven chapters expounding theory and the last five discussing practice. The contemporary teachers of Christians have not only reversed the order, they have inverted the Pauline emphasis on theory and practice. The virtually complete failure of the teachers of the professing church to instruct the faithful in correct doctrine is the cause of the misconduct and cultural impotence of Christians. The Church's lack of power is the result of its lack of truth. The *gospel* is the power of God, not religious experience or personal relationship. The Church has no power because it has abandoned the gospel, the good news, for a religion of experientialism. Twentieth century American Christians are children carried about by every wind of doctrine, not knowing what they believe, or even if they believe anything for certain.

The chief purpose of The Trinity Foundation is to counteract the irrationalism of the age and to expose the errors of the teachers of the church. Our emphasis—on the Bible as the sole source of truth, on the primacy of the intellect, on the supreme importance of correct doctrine, and on the necessity for systematic and logical thinking—is almost unique in Christendom. To the extent that the church survives—and she will survive and flourish—it will be because of her increasing acceptance of these basic ideas and their logical implications.

We believe that the Trinity Foundation is filling a vacuum in Christendom. We are saying that Christianity is intellectually defensible—that, in fact, it is the only intellectually defensible system of thought. We are saying that God has made the wisdom of this world—whether that wisdom be called science, religion, philosophy, or common sense—foolishness. We are appealing to all Christians who have not conceded defeat in the intellectual battle with the world to join us in our efforts to raise a standard to which all men of sound mind can repair.

The love of truth, of God's Word, has all but disappeared in our time. We are committed to and pray for a great instauration. But though we may not see this reformation of Christendom in our lifetimes, we believe it is our duty to present the whole counsel of God because Christ has commanded it. The results of our teaching are in God's hands, not ours. Whatever those results, His Word is never taught in vain, but always accomplishes the result that he intended it to accomplish. Professor Gordon H. Clark has stated our view well:

There have been times in the history of God's people, for example, in the days of Jeremiah, when refreshing grace and widespread revival were not to be expected: the time was one of chastisement. If this twentieth century is of a similar nature, individual Christians here and there can find comfort and strength in a study of God's Word. But if God has decreed happier days for us and if we may expect a world-shaking and genuine spiritual awakening, then it is the author's belief that a zeal for souls, however necessary, is not the sufficient condition. Have there not been devout saints in every age, numerous enough to carry on a revival? Twelve such persons are plenty. What distinguishes the arid ages from the period of the Reformation, when nations were moved as they had not been since Paul preached in Ephesus, Corinth, and Rome, is the latter's fullness of knowledge of God's Word. To echo an early Reformation thought, when the ploughman and the garage attendant know the Bible as well as the theologian does, and know it better than some contemporary theologians, then the desired awakening shall have already occurred.

In addition to publishing books, of which *Education, Christianity, and the State* is the nineteenth, the Foundation publishes a bimonthly newsletter, *The Trinity Review*. Subscriptions to *The Review* are free; please write to the address below to become a subscriber. If you would like further information or would like to join us in our work, please let us know.

The Trinity Foundation is a non-profit foundation tax-exempt under section 501 (c)(3) of the Internal Revenue Code of 1954. You can help us disseminate the Word of God through your tax-deductible contributions to the Foundation.

And we know that the Son of God is come, and hath given us an understanding, that we may know him that is true, and we are in him that is true, in his Son Jesus Christ. This is the true God, and eternal life.

John W. Robbins
President

Intellectual Ammunition

The Trinity Foundation is committed to the reconstruction of philosophy and theology along Biblical lines. We regard God's command to bring all our thoughts into conformity with Christ very seriously, and the books listed below are designed to accomplish that goal. They are written with two subordinate purposes: (1) to demolish all secular claims to knowledge; and (2) to build a system of truth based upon the Bible alone.

Works of Philosophy

Answer to Ayn Rand, John W. Robbins $4.95
The only analysis and criticism of the views of novelist-philosopher Ayn Rand from a consistently Christian perspective.

Behaviorism and Christianity, Gordon H. Clark $5.95
Behaviorism is a critique of both secular and religious behaviorists. It includes chapters on John Watson, Edgar A. Singer Jr., Gilbert Ryle, B.F. Skinner, and Donald MacKay. Clark's refutation of behaviorism and his argument for a Christian doctrine of man are unanswerable.

A Christian Philosophy of Education, Gordon H. Clark $8.95
The first edition of this book was published in 1946. It sparked

the contemporary interest in Christian schools. Dr. Clark has thoroughly revised and updated it, and it is needed now more than ever. Its chapters include: The Need for a World-View, The Christian World-View, The Alternative to Christian Theism, Neutrality, Ethics, The Christian Philosophy of Education, Academic Matters, Kindergarten to University. Three appendices are included as well: The Relationship of Public Education to Christianity, A Protestant World-View, and Art and the Gospel.

A Christian View of Men and Things, Gordon H. Clark $8.95
No other book achieves what A Christian View *does: the presentation of Christianity as it applies to history, politics, ethics, science, religion, and epistemology. Clark's command of both worldly philosophy and Scripture is evident on every page, and the result is a breathtaking and invigorating challenge to the wisdom of this world.*

Clark Speaks From The Grave, Gordon H. Clark $3.95
Dr. Clark chides some of his. critics for their failure to defend Christianity competently. Clark Speaks is a stimulating and illuminating discussion of the errors of contemporary apologists.

Education, Christianity, and the State $7.95
J. Gresham Machen
This is the only collection of Machen's nine essays on Christian scholarship and education. Machen was one of the foremost educators of the twentieth century, and his defense of Christian education and intellectual freedom is even more timely now than it was 50 years ago.

John Dewey, Gordon H. Clark $2.00
Dewey has had an immense influence on American philosophy and education. His irrationalism, the effects of which we can see in government education, is thoroughly critized by Dr. Clark.

Language and Theology, Gordon H. Clark $4.95
Many philosophers and theologians believe language is a barrier to

communication, not an aid. For those who believe in the Word of God, such a view is anathema. Clark analyzes and refutes the language theories of secular and religious philosophers: Bertrand Russell, Ludwig Wittgenstein, Rudolf Carnap, A.J. Ayer, Herbert Feigl, Wilbur Marshall Urban, E.L. Mascall, Horace Bushnell, Langdon Gilkey, William Hordern, and Kenneth Hamilton.

Logic, Gordon H. Clark $8.95
   Written as a textbook for Christian schools, Logic is another unique book from Clark's pen. His presentation of the laws of thought, which must be followed if Scripture is to be understood correctly, and which are found in Scripture itself, is both clear and thorough. Logic is an indispensable book for the thinking Christian.

The Philosophy of Science and Belief in God $5.95
Gordon H. Clark
   In opposing the contemporary idolatry of science, Clark analyzes three major aspects of science: the problem of motion, Newtonian science, and modern theories of physics. His conclusion is that science, while it may be useful, is always false; and he demonstrates its falsity in numerous ways. Since science is always false, it can offer no objection to the Bible and Christianity.

Religion, Reason and Revelation, Gordon H. Clark $7.95
   One of Clark's apologetical masterpieces, Religion, Reason and Revelation has been praised for the clarity of its thought and language. It includes chapters on Is Christianity a Religion? Faith and Reason, Inspiration and Language, Revelation and Morality, and God and Evil. It is must reading for all serious Christians.

Selections from Hellenistic Philosophy, Gordon H. Clark $10.95
   Early in his academic career Clark translated, edited, and commented upon the writings of several philosophers: Lucretius, Zeno of Citium, Chrysippus, Plutarch, Philo Judaeus, Hermes Trismegistus, and Plotinus.

Works of Theology

The Atonement, Gordon H. Clark $8.95
   This is a major addition to Clark's multi-volume systematic theology. In The Atonement, *Clark discusses the Covenants, the Virgin Birth and Incarnation, federal headship and representation, the relationship between God's sovereignty and justice, and much more. He analyzes traditional views of the Atonement and criticizes them in the light of Scripture alone.*

The Biblical Doctrine of Man, Gordon H. Clark $5.95
   Is man soul and body or soul, spirit, and body? What is the image of God? Is Adam's sin imputed to his children? Is evolution true? Are men totally depraved? What is the heart? These are some to the questions discussed and answered from Scripture in this book.

Cornelius Van Til: The Man and The Myth $2.45
John W. Robbins
   The actual teachings of this eminent Philadelphia theologian have been obscured by the myths that surround him. This book penetrates those myths and criticizes Van Til's surprisingly unorthodox views of God and the Bible.

Faith and Saving Faith, Gordon H. Clark $5.95
   The views of the Roman Catholic church, John Calvin, Thomas Manton, John Owen, Charles Hodge, and B.B. Warfield are discussed in this book. Is the object of faith a person or a proposition? Is faith more than belief? Is belief more than thinking with assent, as Augustine said? In a world chaotic with differing views of faith, Clark clearly explains the Biblical view of faith and saving faith.

God's Hammer: The Bible and Its Critics, Gordon H. Clark $6.95
   The starting point of Christianity, the doctrine on which all other doctrines depend, is "The Bible is the Word of God, *and therefore inerrant in the autographs." Over the centuries the opponents of*

Christianity, with Satanic shrewdness, have concentrated their attacks on the truthfulness of the Bible. In the twentieth century the attack is not so much in the fields of history and archaeology as in philosophy. Clark's brilliant defense of the complete truthfulness of the Bible is captured in this collection of eleven major essays.

In Defense of Theology, Gordon H. Clark $12.95
    There are four groups to whom Clark addresses this book: the average Christians who are uninterested in theology, the atheists and agnostics, the religious experientalists, and the serious Christians. The vindication of the knowledge of God against the objections of three of these groups is the first step in theology.

Logical Criticisms of Textual Criticism, Gordon H. Clark $2.95
    In this critique of the science of textual criticism, Dr. Clark exposes the fallacious argumentation of the modern textual critics and defends the view that the early Christians knew better than the modern critics which manuscripts of the New Testament were more accurate.

Predestination, Gordon H. Clark $7.95
    Clark thoroughly discusses one of the most controversial and pervasive doctrines of the Bible: that God is, quite literally, Almighty. Free will, the origin of evil, God's omniscience, creation, and the new birth are all presented within a Scriptural framework. The objections of those who do not believe in the Almighty God are considered and refuted. This volume contains the texts of Biblical Predestination *and* Predestination in the Old Testament.

Scripture Twisting in the Seminaries. Part 1: Feminism $5.95
John W. Robbins
    An analysis of the views of three graduates of Westminster Seminary on the role of women in the church.

The Trinity, Gordon H. Clark $8.95
    Apart from the doctrine of Scripture, no teaching of the Bible is more important than the doctrine of God. Clark's defense of the

orthodox doctrine of the Trinity is a principal portion of a major new work of Systematic Theology now in progress. There are chapters on the deity of Christ, Augustine, the incomprehensibility of God, Bavinck and Van Til, and the Holy Spirit, among others.

What Do Presbyterians Believe? Gordon H. Clark $6.95
This classic introduction to Christian doctrine has been republished. It is the best commentary on the Westminster Confession of Faith that has ever been written.

Commentaries on the New Testament

Ephesians, Gordon H. Clark $8.95
First and Second Thessalonians, Gordon H. Clark $5.95
The Pastoral Epistles (I and II Timothy and Titus) $9.95
Gordon H. Clark
All of Clark's commentaries are expository, not technical, and are written for the Christian layman. His purpose is to explain the text clearly and accurately so that the Word of God will be thoroughly known by every Christian. Revivals of Christianity come only through the spread of God's truth. The sound exposition of the Bible, through preaching and through commentaries on Scripture, is the only method of spreading that truth.

The Trinity Library

We will send you one copy of each of the 26 books listed above for the low price of $125. The regular price of these books is $175. Or you may order the books you want individually on the order blank at the back. Because some of the books are in short supply, we must reserve the right to substitute others of equal or greater value in The Trinity Library.

Thank you for your attention. We hope to hear from you soon. This special offer expires June 30, 1989.

Order Form

Name _____

Address _____

_____

Please: ☐ add my name to the mailing list for *The Trinity Review*. I
             understand that there is no charge for the *Review*.

          ☐ accept my tax deductible contribution of $ _____
             for the work of the Foundation.

          ☐ send me _____ copies of *Education, Christianity and
             the State*. I enclose as payment $ _____.

          ☐ send me the Trinity Library of 26 books. I enclose $125 as
             full payment for it.

          ☐ send me the following books. I enclose full payment in the
             amount of $ _____ for them.

_____

_____

_____

_____

_____

_____

_____

Mail to: The Trinity Foundation
                  Post Office Box 169
                  Jefferson, MD 21755

Please add $1.00 for postage on orders less than $10. Thank you.
For quantity discounts, please write to the Foundation.